A Review of Japanese Management Accounting Literature and Bibliography

Takeo Yoshikawa
(Professor of Information Accounting, Yokohama National University)
Falconer Mitchell
(Professor of Management Accounting, University of Edinburgh)
Jim Moyes
(Lecturer in Accounting, University of Edinburgh)

The Chartered Institute of Management Accountants
63 Portland Place
London W1N 4AB

First published in 1994

ISBN 1 874784 22 1

The publishers of this book consider that it is a worthwhile contribution to discussion, without necessarily sharing the views expressed, which are those of the authors.

No responsibility for loss occasioned to any person acting or refraining from action as a result of any material in this publication can be accepted by the authors or publishers.

Contents

List of Tables

Acknowledgements

The authors' thanks are due to CIMA for funding the research on which this report is based, and to their research and technical department and to its publishing department for their helpful support throughout. Our gratitude is also extended to Caroline Hall who typed the manuscript with great expertise and patience.

Executive Summary

The economic success of Japan has attracted considerable research interest over the last two decades. Much of this has focused on the management methods and strategy of leading corporations, however, and until recently little work had been done on the nature and role of management accounting in Japan.

This report concentrates on this particular aspect of the Japanese commercial situation. It draws together, for researchers, practitioners and educators, the literature which exists on Japanese management accounting. Two sources are used: first, the published Western literature is reviewed (Chapter 2); and second, the indigenous Japanese literature is identified (Appendices 1 and 2) and analysed (Chapter 3).

The work highlights several salient characteristics of Japanese management accounting:

- The underlying philosophy is one of influencing people in accordance with strategic business objectives.
- Management accounting is closely integrated into the management structure, with considerable emphasis on teamwork which is facilitated by job rotation policies.
- A strong emphasis on cost and cost management is evident, with continuous cost improvement a notable feature.
- A rich indigenous management accounting literature exists which requires to be made more accessible to researchers.

This report is intended simply as a first base for those interested in studying Japanese management accounting and as a first step towards improving the accessibility of their indigenous literature on the discipline.

1 Introduction

The success of individual Japanese corporations and of the Japanese economy as a whole has prompted many economic and managerial studies of Japanese business culture and government. Within the business sector these have focused primarily on the economic policies and management methods adopted in Japan, and have thus revealed little about the role which management accounting plays in supplying information to the decision-makers within the Japanese economy. However, within recent years there has been a growing recognition that Western management accountants may also be able to learn from their Japanese counterparts, and the nature of Japanese management accounting has become the subject of a significant number of books and journal papers.

One aim of this report is to bring this material together in a coherent review (see Chapter 2) which summarises the work of both Western researchers examining Japan and Japanese researchers reporting in the Western literature on their country's management accounting philosophies and practices. It thus identifies the main characteristics which this type of literature attributes to Japanese management accounting.

However, it is also concerned with a study of Japanese management accounting literature which is complementary to that outlined above. This involves a more direct examination of Japanese management accounting and has been achieved by reviewing (for the first time in the West, to the best of the authors' knowledge) the recent indigenous Japanese literature on cost and management accounting. This has been done by translating and analysing the subject of papers written in Japanese journals during (approximately) the last decade (see Chapter 3) and by providing a listing of them (see Appendix 2).

The report thus provides a direct view of the topics which comprise the current cost and management accounting literature in Japan. These are compared and contrasted with the Western literature which exists on Japanese management accounting, some conclusions are drawn and ideas for future research floated (see Chapter 4).

This report is therefore intended to provide an initial source of information for those interested in investigating Japanese management accounting and in exploring further the role played by it in the Japanese 'economic miracle'.

2 Western Literature on Japanese Management Accounting

2.1 Introduction

It is only within the last five years that published material on Japanese management accounting has really become common in the West. In the main, publications have been produced by Western researchers although there are now also an increasing number of Japanese academics, often in collaboration with Western co-authors, who are not only visiting the West but also contributing to the Western literature. This chapter reviews this literature by examining the context and purpose of management accounting in Japan, its origins and the nature of its main constituents, i.e. budgeting and control, and decision-making.

2.2 Content and purpose

A number of researchers have stressed the significance of managerial accounting in promoting the efficient and effective management of Japanese organisations. In terms of its basic purpose, management accounting is viewed primarily as a means of encouraging economically desirable behaviour rather than as a discipline concerned simply with the generation of objective financial information. Indeed, Hiromoto (1988) saw the critical difference between the Western and Japanese models of management accounting as stemming from the latter's fundamental concern with influencing the behaviour of people within an organisation rather than simply informing them.

This trait reflects and reinforces a commitment to 'market-driven' management as is shown by Hiromoto's examples of Daihatsu (market-driven accounting practices) and Hitachi (labour-based overhead absorption). Expanding on this idea, Hiromoto highlighted the central principle underlying management accounting in Japan as being the subservience of accounting practice to corporate strategy, i.e. practice should be developed to support strategy. Kharbanda and Stallworthy (1991) confirmed this emphasis and also cited it as the significant determinant of the difference in rationale between Japanese and Western practice. They considered that the most important consequence of the adoption of this approach is the management accountants' appreciation of the advantages of bringing products to market on time, and their consequent emphasis on cost control and non-financial indicators such as lead times at the pre-production stage in the product life cycle.

Kharbanda (1992) provides a more extended analysis of the sources of difference in Japanese and Western management. Five main factors are identified and all relate to emphases which are stressed in Japan:

(i) Universal concern with cost control;

(ii) Cost viewed as a function of selling price;

(iii) Market share rather than ROI as a goal;

(iv) Emphasis on teamwork;

(v) The influencing role of accounting figures.

Together these factors demonstrate the Japanese accountant's ability to integrate management accounting into the fabric of the organisation. It exists to contribute to gaining and maintaining competitiveness in a supportive way. It thus serves the business but is not allowed to dominate control and decision-making.

Hariman (1990), drawing on the work of Hiromoto, outlined the organisational implications and strategic foundations of Japanese management accounting. One of the consequences of the 'influencing' role of management accounting within Japan is that reality is perceived as being less fixed. A more flexible and amorphous approach is taken to information generation which results in a broader view being taken of accounting numbers. Accounting information can therefore become more integrated with 'ideas, strategies and activities' than would be the case in the West. Competitive analysis, for example, requires a blend of hard data and creative thinking, using 'hunch, intuition, common sense, judgement and experience' which is facilitated by the Japanese flexible view of accounting numbers. The job rotation background of the accountant also helps to provide a knowledge base which helps to ensure that financial myopia does not adversely influence decision situations (Yoshikawa et al., 1993).

Morgan and Weerakoon (1989), in a broader study, investigated the differences between Western and Japanese information systems to assess whether those identified might account in some way for the Japanese economic success story. Their conclusion was confirmatory of the above analysis, suggesting that a major advantage was gained by the Japanese focus on market-driven cost systems and cost allocations, which supported manufacturing strategy and integrated employee innovation and effort with long-term goals. Again, they stressed that Japanese costing systems were structured to influence rather than to simply inform.

It was in this context that Munday (1992) saw potential conflict between some of the traditional Western control functions of management accounting and the requirements of strategy – for example, the problems which can occur when cost-driven control devices or performance measures clash with strategic objectives such as achieving quality or delivery targets. However, in order to have a management accounting system which underpins strategy, it is first necessary to have a strategy and for it to be appreciated by the management accounting function. Currie (1990) has suggested that this could be another problem for Western organisations attempting to develop strategically supportive management accounting systems. This is particularly so in respect of advanced manufacturing technology where, in the West, there tends to be a marked lack of strategic awareness combined with inhibiting and inflexible short-term budgetary control systems.

Another important factor influencing both the nature and success of management accounting is the culture of the people involved in the process of providing and using information. Martin et al. (1992) compared both Japanese worker attitudes and Japanese management practices with those prevalent in the USA, and found significant differences in both. Workers in Japan were found to be more loyal, more inclined to co-operate and conform, more nationalistic, with a broader concept of 'self' and with a different attitude towards work, which inclined them to be more receptive to the idea of making sacrifices for the good of the employing company. Moreover, in Japan managers were more accessible, there was greater co-participation in decision-making, employees were seen as a more important resource, from whom suggestions for the improvement of their own performance and of that of the organisation were expected, and incentive systems were based more on psychological factors such as giving recognition for achievement, rather than on mere financial reward. All these attributes facilitate the creation and use of a management accounting system which both reflects strategy and influences behaviour throughout the organisation.

Although many commentators have focused on the advantages of the Japanese systems compared with those of the West, a number have warned of the danger of accepting perceived Japanese approaches as invariably best practice, and uncritically importing them into a different cultural milieu. Bromwich and Bhimani (1989) argue that even if 'firms in the West place greater emphasis on meeting cost objectives than the Japanese, this should not be taken to mean that Western firms are at fault, and ought to adopt the Japanese viewpoint automatically'. Jinnai (1990) gives examples of structural differences which may invalidate any simple comparison between the West and Japan in the lack of 'professionalism' of the accounting function in Japan as compared with Britain and the USA, and in the closer relationships in Japan than in the West between the auditors and the companies they audit. He concludes, 'In constructing a theory of accounting, researchers should consider which characteristics are specific to Japanese capitalism, and which are common to capitalism in all countries.' In relation to the issue of transplanting Japanese techniques into the West, Keys (1991) comments that when in the past Japanese companies borrowed Western techniques, they adapted them to fit into an 'integrated whole' which includes not only the company but also Japanese society, government and the economy. With the greater emphasis on individualism which exists in the USA in comparison with Japan, he expected that the reverse transfer of techniques would be more difficult to successfully implement.

2.3 Context and development

Most current Japanese management accounting practice is of comparatively recent origin. In the main, the systems in use have been introduced since the end of the Second World War. Of particular significance is the interest taken in this area by the government, which throughout the 1950s was active in promoting management accounting guidelines (mainly based on US ideas) which would encourage best practice. The legacy of this remains in the system of cost accounting standards which currently exists in Japan. However, accounting regulation was used in other ways to assist Japanese companies. It enabled the creation of secret reserves within Japanese corporations. Jinnai (1990) argued that the aim of accounting regulation in Japan in this period was not primarily intended to provide fair guidelines for reporting (the guidelines were too flexible), but to constitute 'a crucial part of the state's economic policy through which post-war Japanese capitalism has rapidly developed, centering on the large financial institutions, general trading companies and manufacturers'. He is of the opinion that, in Japan, management and financial accounting are curiously related. The purpose of financial accounting is to conceal or justify the accumulation of monopoly profits earned by the large trading companies, whereas to management accounting falls the role of maximising such profits. Miyagami (1969) supports this view by asserting, 'Business accounting has the function of serving the interests of monopolistic enterprises in reducing corporate tax and in lowering dividends by the mediation of the institutional concept of profit which does not reflect the actual economic profit.'

Managerial developments have also impacted on the nature and role of Japanese accounting. For example, the development of the just-in-time (JIT) system of production has simplified and consolidated the accounting and managerial control functions by bringing together, through the *kanban* system, information flow and physical production. The functions of operational planning, co-ordination and control are all subsumed in the *kanban* system, which is operated by the production workers. Thus a number of what were hitherto viewed as specialised accounting functions are incorporated 'within the everyday activities of the productive workers' (Jinnai, 1990). His conclusions are that Japan provides a good example of a nation where accounting has actually contributed positively to economic growth. He suggests that there is a strong correlation between a backward and loosely regulated system of financial accounting and the use of advanced management control techniques. Indeed, in Jinnai's view, 'they may be regarded as two sides of one coin'.

2.4 Budgeting and control

A comparative survey of management accounting practices in Japan and Scotland carried out by Yoshikawa, Innes and Mitchell (1989) highlights the significant differences between the budgeting and standard costing practices adopted in the two countries. Standard costing was viewed by the Japanese as being of primary importance in stock valuation (for the purpose of financial statement preparation), rather than for cost control. Cost reduction was also seen by the Japanese as being more related to standard costing than it was in the West, and to this aim, revision of standards was undertaken twice as frequently in Japanese companies as in Scottish companies.

Budgeting was a process to which Scottish companies devoted considerable resources. They almost universally produced master budgets for profit and loss accounts, balance sheets, cash flow statements and capital expenditure commitments. Japanese companies, by contrast, tended to produce budgets which in comparison 'evidenced a lack of comprehensiveness'. The only budget statement which was universally produced was the profit and loss account, the other statements only being produced by around 50 per cent of respondents. Japanese budgets were also noted to be less detailed and less frequently revised, with around one-third of companies not revising budgets once they had been set. Surprisingly, only 7 per cent of Japanese companies produced budgets for a period of longer than one year, compared with 42 per cent of the Scottish companies.

Hiromoto (1988) and Monden and Hamada (1991) give insights into the thinking underlying this difference in the context of automobile manufacturers. The former illustrates the practices used by Daihatsu. This corporation has a budgeted or standard cost for a new product at the start of its production, but this cost objective is tightened monthly by a cost reduction rate which is based on short-term profit objectives. In later years, the cost reduction effort is targeted on the actual cost of the previous year.

This continuous striving to reduce actual costs is reflected in the *kaizen* costing described by Monden and Hamada (1991). Hiromoto argues that traditional standard costs reflect an 'engineering mind-set and technology-driven management', whereas what is needed for successful operations is market-driven management, where the question is not how efficiently a product should be built but how efficiently it must be built in order to achieve maximum market-place success. Thus target costs at the product unit level are developed as a function of target prices, and the traditional flexible budget becomes less relevant, or possibly even harmful in that it creates a mind-set which views budget achievement as a satisfactory goal, and neglects the real challenge, which is that of continuous improvement, represented by constantly improving methods and reducing costs. With a more uncertain manufacturing environment, characterised by short lead times, rapid rates of product obsolescence and consequently short life cycles, the utility of traditional standard costing is questionable to the Japanese.

Martin et al. (1992) argue that planning and control in Japanese companies is based on a 'bottom up' model, where there is considerable employee involvement in the development of goals, and significant feedback on goal achievement. They contrast this model with a stereotypical US system, in which budgeting is based on the 'top down' model, and where accounting and control systems have been mainly used to inform managers about company performance. They consider that the Japanese are 'highly committed to planning and feedback' and make extensive use of a plan–do–check–action system through which plans are drawn up, trials run, and evaluation and revisions undertaken, and finally implementation of the proposal takes place. This system satisfies the Japanese need for decisions to be underpinned by supporting documentation.

There is an apparent conflict between the findings of Yoshikawa et al. (1989) that formal master budgets were not accorded great importance, and those of Martin et al. (1992) who found that planning and feedback were an integral part of the Japanese approach to production. However, the two views are reconcilable. Although the Japanese de-emphasise the importance of producing, and updating, formal budgets, these devices are replaced by less formal plans, built at a lower level within the organisation by a lower level of management, and integrated with the overall strategic objectives of the organisation. This is possible because strategy is better communicated downwards and consequently has a greater profile than would be typical in the West.

At the technical level of cost control Inoue (1988) looked at the problems of 'cost down' as experienced by a number of Japanese manufacturing companies. Cost down was defined as an activity which included both cost control and also cost planning. He found that many different techniques were used in pursuit of cost reduction, ranging across both accounting and production methods. The most significant of these techniques, adopted in more than 80 per cent of the companies in his survey, fell under the broad heading of budgetary planning and control. Second in importance was cost planning and cost estimating, third was total quality control. Standard costing came only sixth in importance.

Budgetary planning and control was viewed as the only 'unitary technique which can value company-wide performance'. Inoue saw this as an important link between cost management and profit management. The range of techniques used to identify and effect cost reductions are reviewed by Sakurai (1989) who confirms the establishment of ever reducing cost targets and the utilisation of a variety of both financial and non-financial tools to achieve them. Yoshikawa et al. (1989, 1990, 1993) examine in more detail the use of functional cost analysis (an approach adapted from Western value analysis), cost tables (which provide the basis for quickly quantifying the implications of design changes in financial terms) and target costs, which are all used for continual cost control in Japan.

Tai (1990) examined a number of aspects of the managerial control system of the Matsushita Electric Industrial Company, finding that work was decentralised while control was centralised, these being two of the major characteristics of corporate management. The divisions were controlled, financially, through the use of 'standard balance sheets' which were generated monthly by producing standard values for current assets and liabilities based on the month's turnover. This balance sheet was then compared with the actual balance sheet. The budget system at Matsushita 'has the function of numerically controlling the activities of each section of each operational division, so as to achieve target profits'. The system works on a top down basis, in which top managers set the general guidelines, which are then turned into operational plans (which include the development of new products and measures to reduce production costs) by divisional heads, before final approval by top management. A division's profit plan will be defined by the budget system, which controls activities 'down to the smallest unit of several people on each work level'.

As at Matsushita, the current production environment in many of Japan's most successful industries is characterised by short lead times for the introduction of new products, and by the continuous introduction of new products, which must be sold as part of a wide range of company outputs which are contemporaneously brought to market. With short life cycle products, companies are forced to put more emphasis on product planning, cost planning (target cost) and both basic and detail design.

In this context, Daniel and Reitsberger (1992) compared Japanese and American management control systems, finding significant differences particularly within the area of goal communication to operating managers. Target levels for output and production costs were communicated to Japanese managers almost twice as frequently as to their American counterparts. Ninety per cent of Japanese managers received goals for units of output, and 64 per cent received production cost goals, compared with equivalent figures of 57 per cent and 37 per cent for the American equivalents. It was concluded that the Japanese search for improvements in production output and quality was aided by the clarity and frequency of provision of goals related in these areas to production managers. Furthermore, if operational planning and control mechanisms were not integrated with strategic planning through these regular feedback mechanisms then the significance of the latter will become increasingly eroded over time.

The implication for management accountants was that they will require to become increasingly involved with operations in order to provide meaningful goal-setting and feedback which will allow operational personnel to focus on the actions which will, in turn, improve performance in accord with established strategies. Also on the feedback theme, Anyane-Ntow (1991) tested the assertions of management literature that in comparison with Japanese companies, US manufacturing company executives employ management styles and performance evaluation criteria which place more emphasis on short-term goals, and found that in general the assertions seemed sustainable.

Finally, Bromwich and Bhimani (1989) have viewed cost accounting as a valuable cost control tool for the Japanese companies, which use it to help identify 'new manufacturing methodologies which will produce equivalent or better output with lower resource utilisation'. Costing thus encourages innovation and the development of novel means of production which will improve cost effectiveness and promote the development of new capabilities. The impact of cost accounting is therefore seen as supportive of the factors which are critical to the success of a manufacturing company. Costing has made the transformation from being a rather prosaic means of accumulating and recording cost incurrence to being central to any implementation of operational strategy. It has become a means whereby employee behaviour can be influenced in accord with established strategies.

2.5 Decision-making

Business decisions concerning the usage of resources can be conveniently divided into those with short-term and those with long-term implications. The first type of decision, involving the long term, would, according to the Western doctrine, require discounting techniques to be employed. Kim and Song (1990) surveyed a number of companies in Japan, Korea and the USA, and found that in relation to long-term investment appraisal, the Japanese were, in fact, the least likely to place much emphasis on intuition. They were more concerned with having models to predict decision outcomes. However, these models were most likely to be based on payback period, which ignores both the time value of money and the impact of any cash flows which occur after the payback period has ended. Indeed, 86 per cent of Japanese companies used this approach to investment appraisal, while only 20 per cent used internal rate of return and 28 per cent net present value (a number of companies used more than one technique). This pattern of behaviour is confirmed by Currie (1991a and 1991b) in respect of investments in production technology. Her research identified that a team approach to long-term decision-making was paramount, and non-financial factors were also given a heavy weighting in the decision-making process. These results can be contrasted with those reported in the study by Yoshikawa et al. (1989), which found 52 per cent of Japanese companies using payback, compared with 72 per cent for Scottish companies. However, the Scottish comparators also used net present value and internal rate of return to a significant extent, whereas the Japanese companies effectively concentrated much more exclusively on payback, or accounting rate of return, which also ignores the time value of money. In many ways the greater flexibility and informality of the non-discounting approaches fits the 'behaviour-influencing' emphasis placed on management accounting in Japan. Kharbanda and Stallworthy (1991) support this notion by noting the relative underuse of discounting techniques in Japan, and observing that the normal logic of achieving low unit cost in order to achieve volume and market share goals may in fact be reversed in Japanese investment decisions. In fact, by pursuing market share and volume as a primary objective of decisions, then profit will follow naturally. They view the essence of the Japanese approach to project viability as disregarding standard accounting assessments, and replacing them by an 'entrepreneurial' approach, which is in fact not dissimilar to the Shell plc Direct Policy Matrix (DPM) technique of some years ago. They also argue that a significant advantage accrues to Japanese companies through using this approach as, once approved, implementation of projects is much more rapid. Giving an example of similar facilities being constructed in Japan and in the UK, they note that the much more timely completion in Japan was due to a greater 'concentration and understanding of each other's roles' than in the West.

Although a number of writers have made the point that the Japanese approach to investment choice tends to be much more market driven than that used in the West, it would not be fair to conclude that the Japanese approach, in itself, would be better for a Western company to adopt, for any choice between competing systems must always be considered in context. For example, Bromwich and Bhimani (1989) argue that the Japanese pursuit of long-term growth as opposed to short-term profitability is partly explained by the Japanese financial and organisational infrastructure, in which corporate mutual cross-shareholdings provide a background of financial stability to corporate decision-making and allow a focus on the long term. The Japanese state is also involved in promoting the long-term health of Japanese companies, changing the regulations governing corporate disclosure in 1974 (when the oil price rise shook the developed economies of the world) from semi-annual disclosure to annual disclosure. This had the effect of deferring recognition of the impact of the worsened world economy upon the Japanese corporate sector. The overall effect of Japanese governmental policies and of the corporate interdependences noted above is, according to Bromwich and Bhimani, that 'firms are encouraged to plan their long-term investment relatively free from concerns about reactions from players external to the firm ... and to focus their attention on corporate action that emphasises the long-term well-being of industry, and not just of the individual firm'.

A related issue is the problem which can arise when ownership and control are located other than in the country of operations, a situation which is familiar in much of Western Europe and in the USA and in which conflicts of interest can be significant. Prodhan (1992) concludes that the Japanese–German variety of governance, where property rights and ownership are not widely dispersed, has served these economies well, and may have strengths which causes it to be more appropriate than the US/UK model as the foundation of the developing East European economies. Within the Western economy, where the problems of the short-termism of the capital market are well documented, it may make little sense for an individual firm to depart from a long-term investment appraisal system which is based on cash flows and the rapid recoupment of the initial investment. Indeed, in the context of the early 1990s there is evidence that the 'Japanese policy' of 'buying' market share may be open to criticism in an environment of recession, where slender margins and long-standing policies of competing on price have resulted in many of the major Japanese manufacturing companies suffering substantial losses. For example, Taylor (1993) describes the extensive changes which Toyota have had to make to cope with dropping profitability and global overcapacity in car manufacture.

While the reluctance of Japanese companies to use discounting as a component of their long-term decision-making system differs in emphasis from the Western approach, even more fundamental differences are apparent at the level of shorter-term operational decision-making (for a detailed exposition, see Monden and Sakurai, 1990). These pertain both to the approaches and the systems which are used for this purpose in Japan and the West. Much of the literature in this area contains relatively uncritical 'shopping lists' of items which successful organisations are using. The implication of much of this work is that the transplantation of Japanese practices into a Western environment will result in performance improvement. Thus Howell and Sakurai (1992) write of ten lessons learned from the Japanese. A number of these, such as quick, relevant management reporting, improved measures of performance and world-class customer commitment and feedback might, however, be regarded as general enough to become universal objectives in their own right. Sellenheim (1991), however, links a number of categories of performance measures with the specific promotion of world-class manufacturing as an objective. These include quality, delivery, production process time, flexibility, and finance costs and training. The latter has become a major issue in Japan due to labour shortages. Taylor (1993) notes the greater use of older employees and the continuous recruitment and training of new workers in Toyota. These are caused by an underlying labour turnover rate of 30 per cent for plants in Japan, as opposed to 6 per cent for corresponding plants in the USA. Thus the Japanese situation may result in an emphasis being placed on particular areas and costs which may be less critical at this time in the West.

Worthy (1991) stresses the importance of the Japanese system of forecasting, monitoring and interpreting costs. These activities support continuous operational decision-making which facilitates the production of low-cost products and their speedy introduction to the market. The use of target costs is important, particularly at the planning stage where costs are not committed and can be designed out of the product by a team who are aware of both internal cost patterns and structures and of market conditions (Monden and Hamada, 1991). These targets cover not only capital but also operational-level costs. The Japanese approach of using cost data to trigger, motivate and generate commitment to cost-reduction decisions emphasises a major characteristic of Japanese costing. There is less stress placed on the data precision pursued as a significant aim of Western costing. Thackray (1990) perceived Japanese operational control and decision support systems as being less formal and rigid than those adopted in Britain, while their multiway communications systems were excellent. He saw a trade-off between control and communications, a change in emphasis on one resulting in a requirement for a corresponding change in the other. It may be that an organisation with a strong control system can operate very efficiently in the short term without the benefits of a good system of internal and external communications, but in the longer term the advantages of emphasising communications rather than control may be compelling. He counselled a reduced expectation of significant results from each improvement in method, and a shift in the focus of Western management accounting from measuring results to measuring process improvements achieved.

Williams et al. (1990), also looking at the area of operational management, detected a difference in focus between Japanese and British managers during the 1980s, the former being more concerned with the promotion of good management practices which aid the identification of problems and the implementation of solutions, while in Britain the focus was on the narrower pursuit of labour flexibility. In Japan, at the operational level, management accounting information was adapted to suit the new methods. This idea was reinforced by Jonnson (1990), who found that Japanese managers empower workers not only to undertake but to decide upon the design of the activities they perform and to expect continuous improvement by ceaselessly searching for generators of waste in activities. Operational decision-making was thus being undertaken at operative level largely without the benefit of traditional detailed financial analysis. However, as Monden (1992) has suggested, these decisions are now being supported in Japan by the frequent segmentation of cost accounting into three separate sections: cost control, cost planning, and cost improvement. The latter includes value analysis, value engineering, stimulus and support for operational-level decisions.

Throughout the late 1980s a significant literature developed concerning the features and advantages of the just-in-time or JIT method of production operations, as compared with the traditional 'optimising' systems which had hitherto been the predominant model. The JIT system of production, developed and adopted most prominently by Toyota, contains a number of well-documented features which, according to its advocates, make it useful for both cost reduction and cost control. These include an emphasis on stock reduction, the simplicity and control represented by the *kanban* system, the visibility of operations, the emphasis on quality which is necessary for the system to work, the conversion of 'push' production-led systems into market-driven 'pull' systems, space reduction due to simplification of production organisation and the need for storage, more co-operation between vendors and final assemblers with resulting quality improvements, and a reduced holding cost for such stocks as have to be held. One consequence of the conversion to a JIT production system is that conventional cost accounting systems become obsolete – they are too slow to operate and have difficulty in maintaining a cost flow as rapid as the production flow which is being represented (McNair, Mosconi and Norris, 1988). Moreover, with the increased visibility of productive operations, control can more easily be exercised by managerial observation than through the detailed outputs of a costing system.

2.6 Conclusion

Much has been written about the detailed differences in Japanese and Western management practice. This literature in general supports the contention that the message from Japan is not one of technological superiority. Studies such as that done by Radford (1989) on Japanese involvement in the Dunlop Company have emphasised the importance of organisational and attitudinal change as factors contributing towards performance improvement. In Japan there is no strong tendency to give great emphasis to technological sophistication, but to approach technological investment in a manner firmly rooted in assumptions about how communication systems work, how information flows, how people behave and how they can be motivated. Without an information/relationship theory which embraces both internal and external agents, strategies and goals cannot realistically be set, and potential cannot be determined. The management accounting system is a vital component of a corporate information system, and therefore the information which is communicated through this system has a major influence upon both decision-making and control. The idea of tailoring information to end purposes which involve prompting desired behaviour in accord with strategic objectives appears to underlie much of the development of Japanese management accounting. It is a philosophy which gives supremacy to user needs rather than producer criteria and requirements, and so helps ensure relevance and utility to management accounting.

3
Indigenous Japanese Management Accounting Literature

3.1 Introducion

In Japan an extensive cost and management accounting literature exists. Textbooks are numerous. They comprise not only established Western texts such as Horngren and Foster, Bierman and Drebin, and Kaplan and Atkinson which are widely available both in English and in translated form, but also a large number of indigenous books on the subject. Presently well over one thousand of the latter category are in publication. Appendix 1 provides a listing from the current catalogue of a leading Japanese publisher. Most are standard student texts ranging from introductory to advanced level. The perspectives are varied, to include theory, practice, systems and current practice. Specialist texts are also evident with strategic management accounting, cash flow management accounting, management accounting for R. & D. and profit management all providing interesting niche topics. Even within this one publisher's output there is clear evidence of extensive reader choice and considerable competition. That such variety exists is testimony to the interest in this area which is evident in Japan.

During the period of this study no specialist journals devoted exclusively to cost and/or management accounting existed in Japan. Despite this, a thriving indigenous journal literature exists in these disciplines with almost 800 publications in the nine-year period which was reviewed. This is to be found in three main sources. First, commercial journals that are fairly practical publications aimed at practising managers accounted for more than 10 per cent of publications. Second, professional accounting journals that are published by accounting institutes and again are targeted primarily at a practitioner audience. These accounted for slightly under 10 per cent of publications. Third, academic journals which in Japan are typically published under the auspices of accounting/business/economics subject areas of individual universities (and so provide an exclusive staff outlet for publications). This latter category provides by far the most general source of cost and management accounting publications. In common with the West, most of the literature in all three sources is provided by academic rather than practitioner authors. Table 3.1 summarises how the above factors are reflected quantitatively in the literature surveyed.

Table 3.1 Journal and author type

	n	%
Commercial journal	99	13
Professional journal	51	6
Academic journal	636	81
	785	100
Academic author	780	99
Practioner author	5	1
	785	100

All the papers are listed chronologically in Appendix 2, which also provides an identification of the journal and author type of each.

3.2 The review

The journal publications listing (see Appendix 2) on which this study is based was obtained from a Japanese database called 'NACSIS-IR' which is maintained by the National Centre for Science Information Systems. It covers 900 Japanese journals in the fields of economics, business administration and statistics. All types of accounting fall within the business administration topic heading. The database began in 1983 and had been updated to mid-1991 at the time of the search. Thus the review is based on eight and a half years of publications in these journals. The cost and management accounting listing which was extracted was translated into English mainly by the authors of this paper. Where this was not possible Professor Yoshikawa (joint author of this review) undertook the translation. The publications listing which was generated provided a basis for analysing the nature of the recent indigenous Japanese journal literature on cost and management accounting. The results are provided below.

3.3 General pattern

A numerical analysis of the Japanese papers by topic is contained in Table 3.2. The classification was undertaken by the authors on the basis of the paper's title with reference where necessary to the paper's abstract or content. Appendix 2 contains details of how each paper was categorised. A total of 785 papers were spread over 8 topics which encompass the broad spectrum of the discipline. A particular emphasis is clearly apparent on costing and cost management which accounts for almost one-third of the total output. However, the main topics of management accounting are also evident, with significant contributions on managerial accounting theory and issues (19 per cent), budgeting and control (15 per cent), performance measurement and evaluation (10 per cent) and decision-making (7 per cent). It is also notable that a historical perspective on all aspects of the subject is surprisingly common, with 10 per cent of all papers falling here. The content of each category is explored further below.

3.4 Costing and cost management

In terms of volume this topic dominated the literature, accounting for almost one-third of the papers. In some measure this reflects the fact that cost accounting is a separate specialist area not only in practice but also in Japanese academia, with most university departments having a significant proportion of dedicated cost accounting staff. As Table 3.3 shows, several types of publication were apparent within this general category.

Papers dealing with costing systems and issues formed the most substantial part of the pure costing literature. While a small number of these dealt with conventional job and process costing issues, a large proportion were concerned with the examination of the dynamics of costing systems. They focused on how manufacturing developments such as enhancements in production flexibility, JIT, *kanban*, growth in product variety, the emergence of new products, automation and the use of CIM were influencing and/or should influence costing practice. Moreover, papers on the development of new types of costing system were prominent, e.g. quality costing, life cycle costing and the relationship of value added to costing. In general, the theme of change and development looms large in this section.

The study of other countries' approaches to costing was the second most common subject of publication. It included a

Table 3.2 Aggregate analysis of paper frequencies by year

	1983		1984		1985		1986		1987	
	n	(%)	n	(%)	n	(%)	n	(%)	n	(%)
1. Cost accounting and cost management	8	(18)	21	(31)	26	(26)	21	(31)	26	(46)
2. Management accounting theory and issues	4	(9)	21	(30)	20	(21)	16	(23)	8	(14)
3. Budgeting and control	11	(25)	10	(14)	13	(13)	8	(12)	11	(19)
4. Cost and management accounting history	7	(15)	3	(4)	13	(13)	11	(16)	3	(5)
5. Performance measurement and appraisal	8	(18)	12	(17)	7	(7)	5	(18)	5	(8)
6. Decision-making and planning	3	(7)	3	(4)	15	(15)	4	(6)	1	(2)
7. General empirical studies	–	(–)	–	(–)	–	(1)	3	(4)	1	(2)
8. Cost accounting standards	2	(4)	–	(–)	2	(2)	–	(–)	1	(2)
9. Other	2	(4)	1	(–)	2	(2)	–	(–)	1	(2)
	45	(100)	71	(100)	98	(100)	68	(100)	57	(100)

	1988		1989		1990		1991		Total	
	n	(%)	n	(%)	n	(%)	n	(%)	n	(%)
1. Cost accounting and cost management	38	(29)	46	(38)	38	(32)	23	(39	247	(31)
2. Management accounting theory and issues	24	(19)	20	(14)	21	(18)	11	(19)	145	(19)
3. Budgeting and control	13	(10)	26	(18)	17	(15)	6	(10)	115	(15)
4. Cost and management accounting history	18	(14)	12	(8)	11	(10)	2	(3)	80	(10)
5. Performance measurement and appraisal	10	(8)	12	(8)	16	(14)	3	(5)	78	(10)
6. Decision-making and planning	12	(9)	8	(6)	5	(4)	2	(3)	53	(7)
7. General empirical studies	2	(2)	2	(1)	3	(3)	5	(9)	16	(2)
8. Cost accounting standards	1	(1)	7	(4)	1	(1)	1	(2)	16	(2)
9. Other	10	(8)	11	(8)	3	(3)	6	(10)	35	(4)
	128	(100)	144	(100)	115	(100)	59	(100)	785	(100)

Table 3.3 Costing and cost management publications

	n	%
Costing systems and issues	101	41
International costing studies	40	16
Cost management	40	16
Empirical Japanese studies	20	8
Direct/variable costing	17	7
Particular cost elements	10	4
Software costing	8	3
Joint costs	5	2
Activity-based costing	4	2
Other	2	1
	247	100

specialist paper on new methods of transportation costing in the USA, a US costing case study and five broader survey comparisons of Japanese/US costing (two papers) and Japanese/UK costing (three papers). One further paper examined cost management in Thailand. However, a strong preoccupation with German costing practice was evident from 32 papers on this country's costing and cost management practice. Almost half of these were on the German system of marginal or variable costing. Most were generally descriptive, including one hospital case study, but three focused on specific applications: the establishment of the lower limit to pricing, the use of contribution costing in controlling performance, and the use of 'marginal accounting' for the optimisation of production and sales planning with joint product cost. A further eleven covered a broad range of topics, including the concepts underlying German costing practice, contemporary German costing practice, costing system design, opportunity costing, investment appraisal and cost accounting, taxation and costing and Runnel's 'block cost accounting'.

In more recent years the topic of cost management and strategic management accounting has emerged in the West as a popular topic. It has also emerged as a major area of publication in Japan. The publication listing reveals descriptive, definitional and survey papers set in the Japanese context. However, there are also a range of papers exploring specialist aspects of this topic. Target costing, cost reduction, value engineering, total quality control, and manpower cost management and the role of cost management in production management are all the subject of individual pieces of work which focus on how accounting can contribute to the management of cost. In addition, it is significant that a number of papers within the last two years of the listing focus on the need for a strategic and market orientation in cost analysis.

Also evident in recent years has been a growth in empirical studies of costing in Japan. Only a couple are survey based, the remainder being case studies of particular organisations. They cover a wide range of businesses including electronics, computing, telecommunications, beer, sanitation, ball-bearing manufacture, shipping, postal utility, air cargo, construction, machine manufacture, farming, service firms and non-profit organisations.

While these papers addressed general developments in costing systems, another substantial category of costing publications centred on particular cost elements. These included the conventional broad input classifications of material, labour and overhead. However, more specialised papers were also included on maintenance, distribution, waste, idle capacity and product liability costs. The cost of developing software was also a recurrent subject, attracting particular interest in 1986 and 1987. Two well-established issues in costing – the variable costing alternative and the problem of joint costs – have both attracted some attention. Activity-based costing, which has engendered so many publications in the West, was actually introduced to the Japanese literature in 1986 but only resulted in three more publications during the next five and a half years.

Finally, a mixture of other diverse topics are addressed. These include several reviews of Cooper and Kaplan's work, theory papers on the nature of cost, the relevance of cost to inventory valuation and reviews of current trends and innovations in costing.

3.5 *General management accounting theory and issues*

The influence of the high proportion of academic authors is evident as many of the papers in this category are concerned with general reviews of management accounting at a broad conceptual level. They typically involve terms such as 'conceptual framework', 'essence and function', 'purpose' and 'paradigm'. Others, although still general, are more descriptive, e.g. 'unresolved issues in management accounting' and 'a critical approach to management accounting'. In addition, observations on management accounting practice in Japanese companies are made. The idea of management accounting as a communication system and the behavioural science aspects of the discipline are also explored, and reviews of the significance of the work of Anthony,

Horngren, Kaplan and Mintzberg for the discipline of management accounting are included.

Five other specific areas received consistent attention over the period. Fifteen papers explored the relationship of contingency theory to management accounting. Particular emphasis was evident on the environment and the organisation structure as contingent variables of significance to the nature of management accounting. Although not couched in terms of contingency theory, a further eighteen papers were devoted to exploration of the implications of factory automation and production flexibility development and structural change for the development of management accounting. The application of agency theory to management accounting attracted eight papers during the period. One paper reviews the 'garbage can' model of management accounting. As with the costing publications, there is recent evidence of increasing interest in the strategic dimensions of management accounting. Finally, the focus on Germany is continued here with papers on the adaptability and functions of the discipline in Germany and on 'databank accounting' and the meaning of 'purpose neutral calculation' for management accounting.

3.6 Control and budgets

Again a wide range of topics were covered by the papers falling within this general heading. A variety of themes on this topic were explored. They included a substantial number of papers on the theory and nature of standard costing and more specific individual pieces on statistical cost control, profit and income variances, variance investigation and overhead variances. In addition, three papers dealt with standard costing application to project cost control, to the support of corporate strategy and to its suitability within the context of factory automation. A further seven papers were on the related topic of responsibility accounting. They dealt with general issues, the specific issue of cost controllability (two papers), and empirical studies of how responsibility accounting operates at Volvo.

The need to take a strategic perspective was again evident, with another three papers on strategic budgeting and its role in cost management. Some further interesting practical individual topics were a survey of Japanese budgeting systems, *kaizen* budgeting at Toyota, and the use of operating controls and non-financial indicators in the new manufacturing environment. International comparisons of practice were also made (ten papers) and covered Germany, the USA, the UK and China.

Completing the mix were a series of more academic publications which comprised papers on the application of agency theory to budgeting, behavioural factors with particular emphasis on participation in budget setting, the nature and extent of budgetary slack and the relevance of contingency theory to budgetary practice.

3.7 History

Cost and management accounting history proved to be a subject of substantial and consistent interest over the period of literature analysis. A handful of these papers were general reviews of cost and/or management accounting history but these were supplemented by three other more common types of study. First, the development of particular aspects of the discipline were the focus for several papers. Their subjects included standard costing, direct costing, variable costing, overhead allocation, budgeting and current cost. Second, an international perspective was taken with Canada, Germany, the UK and the USA included as locations for the study of historical developments, standard costing and budgeting being particularly prominent in these studies. These papers included both general studies and more specific work, for example on prime cost and value added in the UK. A number of the international papers also targeted the contribution of individuals such as Hess (break-even chart), Clarke (costs for decision-making), Babbage (cost management), Church (distribution of expense burden) and F. W. Taylor (scientific management and standard costing). Finally, a substantial series of papers (around one-third of the category) examined indigenous Japanese history. These studies almost exclusively focused on individual organisations involved in railways, dockyards engineering companies, dock works and shipbuilding, electronics, military institutions and a university.

3.8 Performance measurement and evaluation

The pre-eminent theme in this category reflected the growth and extent of foreign investment by the Japanese. Twelve papers were concerned with the measurement and evaluation of performance of the overseas subsidiaries of multinational groups. The international dimension was also apparent in a series of eight papers on performance measurement and evaluation practice in Germany, France and the USA.

Some general technical issues on measuring performance were pursued with papers on profit segmentation, cost allocation problems, transfer pricing and the effects of inflation. Behavioural factors focusing on the managerial incentive effects of performance measures, delegation problems and the role of post-decision information were also explored. Only one empirical Japanese study was evident, an electronics company case study. Finally, the contemporary themes of how agency theory relates to internal performance measurement and the integration of the topic with business strategy were the subject of several papers.

3.9 *Decisions and planning*

The composition of this section included a series of rather conventional topics. Relevant costs (including an interesting paper entitled 'A Study of Fixed Costs in Relevant Costing', opportunity costing, cost/volume profit analysis and uncertainty, contribution margin analysis for operational decisions, linear programming, quantitative decision models and pricing all fell into this category. In addition, papers on strategic planning, business planning simulations, cost estimation, activity-based costing for decision-making, and added value and the break-even chart had been published. Some concentration on the relevance of cost and management accounting for managerial decision support systems was apparent, with fourteen papers on this topic. Five papers had an international orientation. These comprised variable costing for decision-making in Germany, pricing in Germany, Schwalenbach's work on cost estimating and pricing, also in Germany, and the nature of US quantitative decision models.

3.10 *General empirical studies*

Relatively few general empirical studies were conducted, although they were becoming more common towards the end of the period of the literature reviewed. They comprised surveys of Australian, Japanese, German, US, Korean, Chinese and French management accounting practice. In addition, several general Japanese cases of management accounting were published. They comprised management accounting in a hospital, railway, farm and in the Japanese multinationals Mitsubishi and Toyota.

3.11 Cost standards

A programme of cost accounting standards has been developed in Japan. The regular publication on this topic throughout the period reflects continuing discussion on the concept of such standards, on the nature of existing and proposed standards and on the impact of those introduced.

3.12 Other

This category contained a few very specialised papers which did not fit into the above categories. They included the review of a distinguished professor's work, laboratory experiments in behavioural accounting, regression analysis for management accounting, and various aspects of social responsibility accounting.

3.13 Conclusion

The foregoing indicates a vigorous and wide-ranging level of activity in the area of cost and management accounting in the Japanese academic community. A strong focus is apparent in the area of cost, cost control and cost management which supports the Japanese emphasis on competitive strength based upon cost-effective production. However, underlying the specific categories of publications identified above are a number of recurring themes which provide an insight into the Japanese approach to the management accounting discipline.

External orientation

Studies of practice in other countries were common and ranged from broad surveys to case studies. During the period under review this international research encompassed Canada, China, France, Germany, Korea, the UK and the USA. Particular emphasis was given to Germany, with a total of 45 papers, the majority of which involved examination of various aspects of costing practice in Germany. Also popular is the analysis of contributions of distinguished overseas academics. The work of Mintzberg, Horngren, Bromwich, Otley, Kaplan, Anthony and Cooper are all included in specific reviews.

Historical studies

A considerable proportion of the papers cited are concerned with the origins and development of techniques not only in Japan but also overseas. These studies cover virtually all the subject topics and are consistent in volume throughout the period. Japanese academic accountants thus evidence a strong willingness to investigate and learn from the past. In part, this factor might be due to a Japanese tradition that some young academics begin their career by finding out about the history of the area in which they wish to specialise.

Strategic perspective

There is evidence that the discipline is viewed as having the potential to contribute to long-term business considerations and to the market positioning of the firm. In this respect the contribution which cost and management accounting can make at a strategic level is evident in some of the papers on cost management, management accounting issues, budgeting, performance evaluation and decision-making.

Theoretical perspective

While a practical bent is apparent in the Japanese literature, current theoretical bases for explaining and analysing various aspects of cost and management accounting appear regularly in the review. Contingency theory is present and examined in relation to general management accounting issues. One contingent variable which was explored in some depth in the costing papers was factory automation, with a series of papers exploring the implications of manufacturing system change (such as CIM, factory automation, *kanban* and JIT) for practice. Agency theory has a more varied application with papers investigating its relevance both in general terms and in the areas of budgeting and control, and performance measurement and evaluation. Finally, the 'garbage can' model of management accounting is the subject of one paper.

Contemporary practical developments

Reviews of recent practical developments in management accounting were also conspicuous. In the costing area quality costing, life cycle costing, software costing systems, and activity-based costing were all subjects covered. Other contemporary topics explored at a practical level included value added and management accounting, value engineering and functional analysis, and the Japanese 'amoeba' approach to performance measurement (this involves the creation of micro profit centres within organisations).

Empirical studies

Although still limited in absolute numbers, a noticeable increase in empirical studies is apparent during the period of the review. While most take the form of surveys (both international and domestic), a handful of case studies have also been conducted.

4
Conclusions

This report has been concerned with an analysis of the literature on Japanese management accounting. This has been achieved firstly by reviewing the main literature published in the West and secondly by an examination of indigenous Japanese publications on the topic. Thus this report is intended to provide an accessible base reference point for those researchers interested in undertaking more specialist studies of the Japanese situation, practitioners interested in finding out more about current practice in Japan, and educators interested in assessing the discipline as it has developed in Japan.

The Western literature suggests that some significant and interesting differences (as compared with the West) exist in both the nature and use of management accounting. In Japan, management accounting is used to service the strategic objectives of the organisation. If market share or low-cost production are critical success factors then the management accounting system will be designed to provide performance measures, control mechanisms and decision support which will both assist in communicating the importance of these factors and actively help employees in their achievement. These processes are further assisted by the close integration of the management accounting function into the managerial team. This, in turn, is facilitated by the job rotation practices of Japanese employment which ensure that management accountants have multidisciplinary experience within their organisation. Thus internal management accounting information is primarily designed to influence behaviour in accord with business objectives. In this respect considerable attention is paid to cost reduction, which is imbued in the Japanese corporate culture. Emphasis is placed on an accounting input at the pre-cost commitment stages where perhaps the major impact can be made on future cost levels. However, continuous cost reduction is also supported through the maintenance of contemporary cost databases and participation in regular value analysis and value engineering exercises.

An extensive indigenous Japanese management accounting literature exists and has been described and listed in this report. It evidences a rich series of studies on Japanese thought and practice.

Within it there is confirmation of the Japanese preoccupation with costs and cost management. However, there is also evidence of awareness of contemporary issues and theory, of attention being paid to the traditional areas of control and performance measurement and decision-making, of the historical origins of the subject and of a willingness to investigate practice and ideas in a wide range of other countries.

It is, however, a literature to which there has been limited access not only because of the language difficulty but also because of the large number of journals throughout which it is dispersed. This report is intended as a first step in improving its accessibility. Further work is required on the translation and publication of selected papers from the Japanese publications already in existence. The authors would be able to provide advice on access to interested parties. During the period of this review publications were located in business and general accounting journals of various types. However, within the last few months the first Japanese journal dedicated to management accounting has been launched. *The Journal of Management Accounting, Japan* is published under the auspices of the relatively new Japanese Association of Management Accountants and contains some English-language papers.

While one must always bear in mind the caveat that the cross-national transplantation of accounting techniques will be greatly influenced by differing cultural, societal and business contacts, the potential to learn from other successful nations is great. Japan has certainly achieved considerable economic success and has done so with a system of management accounting which has some significant differences from the West. Moreover, it has shown that, through modification and adaptation, Western management accounting techniques can be used successfully in another national context. As more becomes known about Japanese management accounting it will be a major challenge for Western accountants to see if this achievement can be reciprocated.

Appendix I Cost and Management Accounting Books from the Current Catalogue of Chuoukeizaisha Publishing Co.

Cost accounting

1 T. Ohota, *Introduction to Cost Accounting.*
2 K. Banba, *Cost Accounting*
3 K. Banba, *Cost Accounting Theory*
4 T. Inoue, *Detail Cost Accounting*
5 K. Sato, *Cost Accounting Theory*
6 S. Aoki, *New Cost Accounting*
7 S. Aoki, *Cost Accounting Exercises*
8 S. Aoki (ed.), *A Study on Cost Accounting Theory Based on References*
9 K. Mizoguchi, *New Cost Accounting by Illustrations*
10 K. Mizoguchi, *New Cost Accounting Lecture*
11 K. Mizoguchi, *Cost Accounting: Understandable for Everybody*
12 K. Mizoguchi and M. Ryotou (translation), *Direct Costing*, by H.G. Cruse
13 S. Sato, *Modern Cost Accounting*
14 S. Sato, *Managerial Cost Accounting*
15 Y. Kobayashi, *Cost Accounting for Planning*
16 O. Nishizawa, *Cost Accounting*
17 O. Nishizawa, *Cost Accounting for Distributions*
18 K. Kobayashi, *Modern Cost Accounting Theory*
19 K. Kobayashi, *The History of Cost Accounting*
20 K. Kobayashi, *Direct Costing Based on References*
21 H. Sonoda, *Direct Costing Based on J.N. Harris*
22 K. Kobayashi and M. Kawahara, *Fundamental Cost Accounting*
23 M. Tumagari, *The Lecture of Cost Accounting Theory*
24 M. Tumagari and T. Miyamoto (eds), *Fundamental Knowledge of Cost Accounting*
25 M. Miyamoto, *Cost Accounting Systems*
26 M. Miyamoto, *Cost Accounting Theory*

27 T. Kobayashi, *Cost Accounting*
28 S. Sato, *Lucid Explained Cost Accounting*
29 S. Sato, *Detail Standard Cost Accounting*
30 S. Sato, *Management and Calculation of Costs*
31 Y. Kijima, *Institutional Cost Accounting Theory*
32 K. Kadoya, *Fundamentals of Modern Cost Accounting*
33 K. Kadoya, *Modern Cost Accounting*
34 H. Yazawa and T. Sato, *Basic Cost Accounting*
35 H. Kaneko, *Tabulating Cost Accounting*
36 Usui. Kikutani and Yamaguchi, *Introductory Modern Cost Accounting Theory*
37 Y. Harada (ed.), *Fundamental Cost Accounting*
38 L. Shikita, *New Cost Accounting Theory*
39 T. Ohnishi, *Practical Cost Accounting*
40 M. Sakurai, *Managerial Cost Accounting Theory*
41 S. Shimizu, *Detail Managerial Cost Accounting*
42 S. Shimizu, *Detail Cost Accounting Theory*
43 K. Matuo, *Cost Accounting Theory*
44 Khono, *Cost Accounting and Price Decision*
45 Y. Harada and Y. Kojima, *Detail Industrial Accounting*
46 K. Yamagata, *A Study on Cost Theory*
47 K. Mizoguchi (translation), *Cost Theory*, by Hynen

Management accounting

48 K. Okamoto (ed.), *Fundamental Knowledge of Management Accounting*
49 S. Sato, *Introduction to Management Accounting*
50 K. Banba, *Cost Management Accounting*
51 S. Aoki, *A Study on Management Accounting*
52 K. Mizoguchi (ed.), *A Study on Management Accounting Theory*
53 K. Mizoguchi, *Expense Management Theory*
54 O. Nishizawa, *Management Accounting Theory*
55 K. Mizoguchi (ed.), *Fundamental Management Accounting*
56 K. Tuji (ed.), *Fundamental Theory of Management Accounting*
57 K. Takahashi, *Modern Management Accounting*
58 T. Tanaka (ed.), *Modern Management Accounting Systems*
59 S. Sato and T. Yoshikawa (translation), *Management Accounting*, by Bierman and Drebin
60 A. Nishimura and S. Kon (translation), *Advanced Management Accounting*, by Kaplan
61 H. Yanagita, *Management Accounting Theory in Germany*
62 Y. Monden and S. Inoue (translation), *Management Accounting of the 90s'*, by Johny Lee
63 Accounting Research Room in Kobe University (ed.), *Modern*

Management Accounting Theory
64 K. Someya (ed.), *Modern Management Accounting Theory*
65 K. Adachi, *Management Accounting Research: A Study on R. & D. Management*
66 K. Moroi (ed.), *Modern Decision-making Accounting*
67 Y. Sakamoto (ed.), *Modern Business and Management Accounting*
68 S. Sato (ed.), *Development of Modern Management Accounting*

69 T. Fushimi, *Business Strategic Management Accounting*
70 M. Miyamoto, *Accounting Information and Decision-making*
71 Y. Masutani, *Analytical Accounting Theory*
72 K. Miyamoto, *Fundamentals of International Management Accounting*
73 K. Miyamoto, *Management Accounting for Multinational Companies*
74 T. Furuta, *Performance Management Accounting*
75 S. Nakahara (ed.), *Business Finance and Management Accounting*
76 Y. Kobayashi, *Business Behaviour and Management Accounting*
77 Toyou Accounting Firm (ed.), *Practice of Internal Management*
78 K. Mizoguchi, *Introductory Profit Management Handbook*
79 A. Shiba, *Management Accounting Knowledge for Practices*
80 A. Koike, *Profit Management Methods in NEC*
81 K. Kadoya, S. Tunashima and H. Yamada, *Foundations of Budgetary Control*
82 E. Aho, H. Ishizuka and U. Maeda, *Modern Business Budget*
83 K. Kondou, *Budgeting Theory*
84 K. Kobayashi, *Sales Forecast for Profit and Budgeting*
85 S. Shinada, *Cash Flow Management Accounting*
86 H. Fukai, *Dynamic Cost Management*
87 S. Sato, *Cost Accounting for Profit Management*
88 S. Sato, *Cost Policy*
89 S. Shimizu, *Cost Information Transmission Theory*
90 K. Kadoya, *Management of Administration Expenses*
91 S. Sato, *Cost Accounting for Managerial Engineers*
92 N. Matuo, M. Nakamura and M. Matuo, *Planned Economy and Self-supporting Accounting System*
93 Accounting Research Room in Kobe University, *Handbook of Management Accounting*

Note: All the above titles were translated from Japanese for this monograph.

Appendix 2
Indigenous Japanese Journal Publications

Coding Key:

Author	AA	Academic author
	PA	Practitioner author
Publication	AJ	Academic journal
	CJ	Commercial journal
	PJ	Professional journal
Subject	1	Cost accounting and cost management
	2	Control and budgeting
	3	Management accounting theory and issues
	4	Cost and management accounting history
	5	Performance measurement and appraisal
	6	Decision-making and planning
	7	General empirical studies
	8	Cost accounting standards
	9	Other
Title	T	Our translation of the original title
	O	Original title translated by the paper's author

1983

1 Teruhiko Suzuki and Yasumasa Konda, 'The Fundamental Attribution Error in Japan and American Performance Appraisal Processes', *The Doshisha Business Review*, 1983, 9. AA,AJ,5,O

2 Yutaka Hayakawa, 'Transfer of Cost Accounting Standards Board', *Accounting*, 1983, 10. AA,AJ,8,O

3 Sadayoshi Maeda, 'A Fundamental Research on Uniform Cost Accounting System and CASB', *The Journal of Musashi University*, 1983, 10. AA,AJ,8,O

4 Norio Nakada, 'Die Entwicklung der Grenzkostenrecknung West Deutschland (A) – Die Teilkostenrecknung auf variablen Kosten' *['The development of marginal costing in West Germany']*, *The Journal of Ryutsu Keizai*, 1983, 7. AA,AJ,1,O

5 Yoshio Tanaka, 'The Real State of Application of Direct Costing in Japan since 1975', *The Kagawa University Economic Review to Professor Masashi Kumura in appreciation of his many years of service*, 1983, 6. AA,AJ,1,O

6 Tatsuhiko Arakawa, 'Foundation of Labor Costing in Japan', *Keirichishiki*, 1983, 3. AA,CJ,1,T

7 Yukio Harada, 'A Review on Performance Appraisal Accounting – Based on Group Management', *Accounting*, 1983, 10. A A,AJ,5,O

8 Yasutaka Hasegawa, 'CVP Analysis and "Uncertainty" – Literature Survey', *The Journal of Business and Economics*, 1983, 3. AA,AJ,6,O

9 Katsuro Hirano, 'Performance Evaluation and Price Level Changes', *The Journal of the Research Institute of Business Administration*, 1983, 7. AA,AJ,5,O

10 Tadashi Itagaki, 'Construction of Performance Through Management Accounting', *Yamaguchi Journal of Economics and Business Administration*, 1983, 5. AA,AJ,5,O

11 Yoshihiro Ito, 'The Contemporary Issues of Responsibility Accounting', *The Journal of Business and Economics*, 1983, 9. AA,AJ,2,O

12 Masao Matsumoto, 'Introduction to the Theory of Cost Management', *Tokyo International University Ronso*, 1983, 9. AA,AJ,1,T

13 Shinobu Muramatsu, 'Performance Evaluation of Junior Companies for Group Management', *Sangyokeiri*, 1983, 10. PA,PJ,5,T

14 Takazu Nakase, 'Management Accounting as a Communication System', *Accounting*, 1983, 9. AA,AJ,3,O

15 Koichi Saito, 'The Controllability and Performance Evaluation Criteria in Responsibility', *The Journal of Business and Economics*, Graduate School of Commerce, Waseda University, 1983, 9. AA,AJ,5,O

16 Michiharu Sakurai, 'ROI and Japanese Economic Growth', *Kigyokaikei*, 1983, 10. AA,CJ,5,T

17 Hiromitsu Sato, 'The Usefulness of Managerial Accounting Information under Multi-person Setting: Some Tests Based on Agency Model (1)', *The Waseda Journal of Social Sciences*, 1983, 7. AA,AJ,3,O

18 Hiromitsu Sato, 'Budget Participation under Information Asymmetry (1, 2)', *Accounting*, 1983, 8; 1983, 9. AA,AJ,2,O

19 Susumu Sato, 'The Concept of Cost Management', *Kigyokaikei*, 1983, 8. AA,CJ,1,T

20 Kazumichi Suzuki, 'The Framework of Management Accounting – R.N. Anthony's Management Accounting

Theory', *Kaizai Ronshu*, Daitobunka University, 1983, 9. AA,AJ,3,T

21 Akira Yoshida, 'A Management Accounting Approach to Capital Budgeting', *Accounting*, 1983, 11. AA,AJ,2,O

22 Hiroyoshi Yabe, 'Measurement of the Quality of Life and Social Cost Accounting', *Accounting*, 1983, 11. AA,AJ,9,O

23 Koichi Sumiya, 'Introduction to Project Cost Control', *Meiji Business Review*, 1983, 10. AA,AJ,2,O

24 Isao Yamada, 'Accounting Significance of Top Management's Performance Evaluation in the USA', *The Journal of Gifu College of Economics*, 1983, 12. AA,AJ,5,O

25 Fumio Yoshimura, 'An Analysis of the Management Aspect of Budgeting', *Economic Review*, Kanazawa University, 1983, 10. AA,AJ,2,O

26 Yoshitaka Kijima, 'On Clark's Theory of "Different Costs for Different Purposes"', *The Journal of Commerce*, Chuo University, 1983, 7. AA,AJ,4,O

27 Yoshitaka Kijima, 'On the Basis of Clark's Theory of Cost Concept', *The Journal of Commerce*, Chuo University, 1983, 9. AA,AJ,4,O

28 Tsugio Kono, 'Die Kostenzurechnung mit dem Kostenverursachnungsprinzip und Nachrichtrechnung (1) - uberlegung des Direct Costings' *['Cost allocation based on the principle that variable costs must be traced to the cost centres and costing units where they originated'], Oita Daigaku Economic Review*, Oita University, 1983, 9. AA,AJ,1,O

29 Keiichi Numa, 'Contribution Margin in Operational Decision-making', *Keieironso*, Nihon University, 1983, 10. AA,AJ,6,O

30 Hiroshi Torii, 'Continuous Process Cost System', *The Papers and Proceedings of Economics*, 1983, 12. AA,AJ,1,O

31 Yoshikazu Toyoshima, 'Some Comments on Letters to the Manager of Nagasaki Dockyard and Engine Works in 1885–1887', *Annual Report of the Economic Society*, Tohoku University, 1983, 11. AA,AJ,4,O

32 Junzo Wada, 'Some Notes on the Development of Standard Costing (2) – On the Cost Analysis of G.C. Harrison', *Business Review*, Tohoku University, 1983, 11. AA,AJ,4,O

33 Hitoshi Yanagita, 'Grundbegriffe der modernen Kostenrechnung' *['Basic concepts of modern cost accounting'], The Nagoya Gakuin University Review*, 1983, 12. AA,AJ,1,O

34 Hironasa Itani, 'Cost Accounting for Decision-making and Relative Variable Costing in West Germany', *Shogaku Kenkyu Nenpo*, Senshu University, 1982, 3. 1983, 3. AA,AJ,6,T

35 Masanobu Kosug, 'The Alternative to Budgeting', *Journal of*

Business Administration of Kwansei Gakuin University, 1983, 12. AA,AJ,2,O

36 Michiharu Sakurai, 'A Comparative Study on Management Accounting Practices in Japan and the USA', *Senshu Keieigaku Ronshu*, 1983, 7. AA,AJ,3,T

37 Masao Sato, 'An Evaluation of Babbage's Achievements in Cost Management', *Chiba University of Commerce Review*, 1983, 9. AA,AJ,4,T

38 Kouji Yamamoto, 'Performance Evaluations and Cost Variance Analysis in Production Departments: An Implication of Statistical Cost Control Models', *Kagawa University Economic Review*, 1983, 12. AA,AJ,2,O

39 Fumio Nezu, 'Introductory Steps for Social Accountabililty Study', *The Bulletin of the Faculty of Commerce*, Meiji University, 1983, 10. AA,AJ,9,O

40 Kazuo Arai, 'Problems in Budgeting, Path Goal Theory and SEU Model', *Studies in Humanities* (Humanities and Economics), 1983, 10. AA,AJ,2,O

41 Takayuki Asada, 'A Budgeting System and Contingency Theory', *Shogaku Ronshu*, Fukushima University, 1983, 3. AA,AJ,2,T

42 Susumu Ito, 'Accounting Processes and Characteristics for Short-run Profit Planning and Control', *Papers of the Research Society of Commerce and Economics*, 1983, 12. AA,AJ,2,O

43 Shinichi Korogi, 'An Industrial Background of Management Accounting Development in USA – American Feature in the Railway Age', *Nakakyushu Junior College Ronso*, 1983, 11. AA,AJ,4,T

44 Shinichi Korogi, 'An Industrial Background of Management Accounting Development in the USA – American Features from the Revolutionary War to the 1930s', *Nakakyushu Junior College Ronso*, 1983, 7. AA,AJ,4,T

45 Masatoshi Uchida, 'Foundational Theory of Budgetary Management', *Hokkai-Gakuen University Journal of Economics*, 1983, 12. AA,AJ,2,O

1984

1 Hiroshi Sakaguchi, 'The Empirical Study on Motivational Function of Budgeting – The review of the work by D.G. Searfoss', *Josei University Bulletin*, 1984, 2. AA,AJ,2,T

2 Kazuo Mizoguchi, 'Review of Japanese Cost Accounting Standards', *Kigyokaikei*, 1984, 1, 3. AA,CJ,1,T

3 Kanui Miyamoto, 'A Study on Performance Evaluation of Overseas Junior Companies, Focusing on Foreign Currency

Exchange Issues', *Osaka Gakuin Shogakuronso*, 1983, 1. AA,AJ,5,T

4 Yoshihiro Hirabayashi, 'A Study on Materials of Costing in Lobnitz & Company Limited', *Business Review*, Osaka City University, 1984, 1. AA,AJ,1,O

5 Norio Nakada, 'Die Entwicklung der Grenzkostenrechnung in West Deutschland (B) – Die Teilkostenrechnung auf relativen Einzelkosten (1)' *['The development of marginal costing in* West *Germany'], The Journal of Ryutsu Keizai University*, 1984, 1. AA,AJ,1,O

6 Masaki Miyamota, 'Management Accounting and Organisational Structure', *Accounting*, 1984, 2. AA,AJ,3,T

7 Hiromitsu Sato, 'An Analysis of Management Accounting Information Based on Agency Model', *Accounting*, 1984, 2. AA,AJ,3,T

8 Muneya Sato, 'A Change of Organisational Structure and Management Accounting', *Accounting*, 1984, 2. AA,AJ,3,T

9 Makoto Takewaki, 'The Usefulness of Overhead Cost Allocation', *Fudai Keizai Ronshu*, 1984, 3. AA,AJ,1,T

10 Takeyuki Tani, 'Organisational Structure and Management Accounting Information – Focusing on Setting Transfer Prices and Allocation of Headquarter Expenses', *Accounting*, 1984, 2. AA,AJ,3,T

11 Daisuke Watanabe, 'Management Accounting in Britain during the Nineteenth Century', *Osaka Keidai Ronshu*, 1984, 3. AA,AJ,4,O

12 Yukio Harada, 'A Study on SBU and Performance Evaluation Based on Divisional Organisation', *Accounting*, 1984, 4. AA,AJ,5,T

13 Mitsuhiro Masaoka, 'The Usefulness of Participative Budgetary Management in Japanese Enterprises', *The Journal of Economics and Business Studies of Ryukoku University*, 1984, 3. AA,AJ,2,O

14 Tetsuo Kobayashi, 'Cost Accounting Systems for Adaptive Budgetary Control', *Accounting*, 1984, 7. AA,AJ,2,O

15 Akihiro Saki, 'Uber die Grenzplankostenrechnung – mit besondere Bezug auf die Theorie von Seicht' *['Concerning standard direct costing – with reference to the theory of Seicht'], Meiji Accounting Review*, 1984, 3. AA,AJ,1,O

16 Tadashi Shimura, 'On the Design of Cost Accounting Systems and Applications of the Framework of Contingency', *The Review of Business Administration*, 1984, 4. AA,AJ,3,O

17 Takanori Furuta, 'An Expectancy Theory Approach to Accounting of Performance Control (1), (2)', *Accounting*, 1984, 6. AA,AJ,2,O

18 Hiroshi Ito, 'A Study on Behavioural Science in Budgeting',

Mita Keizaigaku Kenkyu, Keio University, 1984. AA,AJ,2,T

19 Haruzo Kaneko, 'Japanese Features of Management Accounting for Performance Evaluation', *Kigyokaikei*, 1984, 5. AA,CJ,5,T

20 Kobayashi Tetsuo, 'The Concept of Controllability in Responsible Accounting', *Kokumin Keizaizasshi*, Kobe University, 1984, 5. AA,AJ,2,T

21 Jun Nagaoka, 'A Study on the Framework of Management Accounting', *The Fujironso* (Studies in Economics, Business Administration and the Liberal Arts), Fuji Junior College, 1984, 5. AA,AJ,3,O

22 Akira Nishimura, 'The Theory of Standard Costing Development and Criticism – Management Accounting Development and a Theory of Variance Analysis', *Keizaigaku Kenkyu*, Kyushu University, 1984, 3. AA,AJ,2,T

23 Yasuyuki Ono, 'Managerial Incentive Effects of Performance Evaluation Information', *Meiji Accounting Review*, 1984, 3. AA,AJ,5,O

24 Kyosuke Sakate, 'On the Alternative Theory Approaches in the Managerial Accounting Research', The Review of Business Administration, *Soka University*, 1984, 3. AA,AJ,3,O

25 Hiromitsu Sato, 'The Usefulness of Managerial Accounting Information under Multi-person Setting: Some Tests Based on Agency Model (2)', *The Waseda Journal of Social Sciences*, 1984, 3. AA,AJ,3,O

26 Yasuo Sato, 'Management Accounting and Behavioural Science Implications Research Methodology', *The Hosei Journal of Business*, 1984, 4. AA,AJ,3,O

27 Kazumichi Suzuki, 'The Relationship Between Management Accounting and Financial Accounting', *Keizai Ronshu*, Kaitobunka University, 1984, 3. AA,AJ,3,T

28 Takeyuki Tani, 'Management Accounting Systems and Interdependency Management', *Kokumin Keizai Zasshi*, Kobe University, 1984, 2. AA,AJ,3,T

29 Jusaku Ushio, 'Management Accounting and Pricing Decisions', *Shokei Ronshu*, Chiba Economic Junior College, 1984, 4. AA,AJ,6,T

30 Hajime Yasukuni, 'Environmental Correspondence and Performance Evaluation of Production Department', *Sangyokeiri*, 1984, 4. AA,AJ,5,T

31 Susumu Sato, 'System and Cycle of Cost Management', *The Journal of Commerce*, Chuo University, 1984, 1. AA,AJ,1,O

32 Daisuke Watanabe, 'Financial Accounting and Management Accounting', *Osaka Keidai Ronshu*, 1984, 6. AA,AJ,3,O

33 Isao Iisuka, 'Re-examination of Marple's View on the Nature of Direct Costing', *Accounting*, 1984, 9. AA,AJ,1,O

34 Michio Nakamura, 'Classification of Standard Costing in the DDR', *Meidai Shogaku Ronso*, Meiji University, 1984, 2. AA,AJ,2,T

35 Fumiyasu Takahashi, 'The Purpose of Cost Accounting and Cost Accounting Systems', *Kaikeigaku Kenkyu*, Nihon University, 1984, 6. AA,AJ,1,T

36 Hitoshi Yanagida, 'Die Vargeschichte der Modernen Kostenrechnung' *['The prehistory of modern cost accounting'], The Nagoya Gakuin University Review*, 1984, 3. AA,AJ,4,O

37 Teruyoshi Kitamura, 'Performance Evaluation from a Behavioural Science Perspective', *Sangyokeiri*, 1984, 7. PA,PJ,5,T

38 Kengo Kobayashi, 'Cost Management and Performance Evaluation – Classification of Accounts Based on Responsibility', *Sangyokeiri*, 1984, 7. AA,PJ,5,T

39 Yasumasa Kondo, 'Cost-Benefit Analysis in Management Accounting', T*he Doshisha Business Review*, 1984, 6. AA,AJ,3,O

40 Takao Makido, 'A Measurement of Cost Performance in the Case of Cost Alternative Possibilities', *Sangyokeiri*, 1984, 7. AA,PJ,1,T

41 Masao Matsumoto, 'The Concept of Cost Management and Cost Performance Evaluation', *Sangyokeiri*, 1984, 7. AA,PJ,1,T

42 Masaaki Miyamoto, 'The Relationship Between Cost Management and Performance Evaluation', *Sangyokeiri*, 1984, 7. AA,PJ,1,T

43 Hidekazu Nomura, 'J. Lee Nicholson's Theory of Cost Management', *The Economic Review*, Kyoto University Economic Society, 1984, 8. AA,AJ,1,O

44 Seizo Ozeki, 'New Trends of Performance Evaluation in France', *Kigyokaikei*, 1984, 10. AA,CJ,5,T

45 Yoshiho Tanaka, 'Production Methods and the Types of Cost Accounting of Japanese Manufacturing Companies in 1982', *The Kagawa University Economic Review*, 1984, 6. AA,AJ,1,O

46 Sohei Hibi, 'Cost Management in Thailand', *Aoyama Journal of Business*, 1984, 9. AA,AJ,1,O

47 Seiichi Sato, 'Comparative Research on the Managerial Accounting Literature in America', *Yokohama Business Review*, 1984, 12. AA,AJ,3,O

48 Akira Yoshida, 'An Approach to a Development of Management Accounting Information', *Accounting*, 1984, 11. AA,AJ,3,O

49 Isao Iizuka, 'Re-examination of Marple's View on the Nature of Direct Costing', *Accounting*, 1984, 12. AA,AJ,1,O

50 Tadashi Kanai, 'A Memorandum on Costing and Added Value Accounting', *Journal of Law and Economics*, Iwate Prefectural Morioka College, 1984, 12. AA,AJ,1,O

51 Tsugio Kono, 'Die Kostenzurechnung mit dem Kostenverursachnungs – prinzip und Nachrichtrechnung (2) – Eine Uberprufung des Direct Costings' *['Cost allocation on the principle by which variable costs must be traced to cost centres and cost units where they originated – An examination of direct costing'], Oita University Economic Review*, 1984, 1. AA,AJ,1,O

52 Norio Nakada, 'Die Entwicklung der Grenzkostenrechnung in West Deutschland (B) - Die Teilkostenrechnung auf relativen Einzelkosten (2)' *[The development of marginal costing in West Germany – On relative direct costs'], Yamaguchi Journal of Economics, Business Administration and Law*, 1984, 7. AA,AJ,1,O

53 Michio Nakamura, 'Development of "Normative Kostenrechnung" in the GDR' *[Development of standard cost accounting in East Germany'], Accounting*, 1984, 12. AA,AJ,2,O

54 Heizaburo Sonoda, 'The "Multi-Margin Approach and Multi-Block System" in Direct Costing', *Shogaku Shushi*, Nihon University, 1984, 12. AA,AJ,1,O

55 Takeo Yoshikawa, 'An Empirical Study and a Model Building of a Process Cost Accounting System by Non-Cumulative Methods', *Yokohama Business Review*, 1984, 12. AA,AJ,1,O

56 Shigeo Aoki, 'The Modern Role of Departmental Performance Evaluation Accounting', *Zeimutsushin*, 1984, 12. AA,CJ,5,T

57 Shuzo Kamijo, 'Towards a Contingency Approach to Management Accounting – On the Ansari Study', Tokyo Metropolitan Junior College of Commerce, 1984, 8. AA,AJ,3,O

58 Sadao Mitsuoka, 'Opportunity Costs and Cost Accounting for Decision-making (1), (2)', *Konan Business Review*, 1984, 9; 1985, 1. AA,AJ,6,O

59 Hiromitsu Sato, 'The Usefulness of Management Accounting Information Under Multi-person Setting: Some Tests Based on Agency Model (3)', *The Waseda Journal of Social Sciences*, 1984, 9. AA,AJ,3,O

60 Kazuyuki Suda, 'A Profit Segment Indication and Performance Evaluation in Current Cost Accounting', *Sangyokeiri*, 1984, 10. AA,PJ,5,T

61 Naohisa Sueishi, 'New Challenges for Management Accounting Research – A Review of R.S. Kaplan's Article', *The Review of the Osaka University of Commerce*, 1984, 12. AA,AJ,3,O

62 Takao Tanaka, 'A Performance Evaluation Index of Investment Centre Focusing on the Effectiveness of ROI', *Sangyokeiri*, 1984, 10. AA,PJ,5,T

63 Shiro Inamoto, 'On Agriculture Management Accounting and Linear Programming', *Nogyo Keizaigaku Kenkyu, Kyoto University*, 1984, 10. AA,AJ,6,T

64 Yasuo Inoue, 'Joint Products, By-products and Spoiled Units in Process Cost Accounting', *The Commerce Review of Seinan Gakuin University*, 1984, 11. AA,AJ,1,O

65 Tsugio Kono, 'Die Anpassungsfahigkeit des Zwecks fur "Grundrechnung" als Managerial Accounting' *['The adaptability of basic accounting as managerial accounting'], Oita University Economic Review*, 1984, 9. AA,AJ,3,O

66 Ichiro Mizuno, 'A Study of Management Accounting', *Keizaigaku-Ronshu of Kagoshima University*, 1984, 12. AA,AJ,3,O

67 Bokuryo Nagahama, 'The Basic Problems of the Management Accounting', *Economic Papers*, 1984, 12. AA,AJ,3,O

68 Hisao Miyai, 'Scientific Management and Standard Cost Accounting', *Okinawa University Economic Review*, 1984, 10. AA,AJ,2,O

69 Tadashi Shimura, 'The Measurement of Investment Base for Calculating FOI and RI Measures under Inflation', *The Review of Business Administration, Soka University*, 1984, 11. AA,AJ,5,O

70 Susumu Ito, 'CASB's Cost Accounting Procedures', *Papers of the Research Society of Commerce and Economics*, Hiroshima Shudo University, 1984, 12. AA,AJ,8,O

71 Shinichi Korogi, 'An Industrial Background of Management Accounting Development in the USA – American Feature in the Scientific Management Ages', *Nakakyushu Junior College Ronso*, 1984, 12. AA,AJ,4,T

1985

1 Kazuyoshi Kumura, 'The Effective PC Database for Making Management Accounting Information', *Kigyokaikei*, 1985, 2. AA,CJ,3,T

2 Saburo Kameyama, 'The Development of Management Accounting Systems – Accounting and Industrial Management Approaches', *Kigyokaikei*, 1985, 1. AA,CJ,3,T

3 Yoshihiro Hirabayashi, 'Cost Accounting in Germany in the Nineteenth Century – Abstract from "Betriebsbnchhaltung und industrielle Selbstkostenrechnung in 19 Jahrhundert"', *Business Review*, 1985, 1. AA,AJ,4,O

4 Yasuhiro Kadota, MRP, 'Integration of the *Kanban* System and Cost Accounting', *Kigyokaikei*, 1985, 2. AA,CJ,1,T

5 Masaaki Miyamoto, 'A New Subject of Cost Accounting', *Kigyokaikei*, 1985, 3. AA,CJ,1,T

6 Masahiro Nakayama, 'The History of Cost Accounting

Standards in Japan', *Senshu Keieikenkyu Nenpo*, 1985, 2.AA,AJ,4,T

7 Yasumi Sakamoto, 'A Study on Cost Accounting for the Environmental Sanitation Business', *Zyochi Keizai Ronshu*, 1985, 3. AA,AJ,1,T

8 Muneya Sato, 'Cost Accounting for the Telecommunication Business', *Accounting*, 1985, 1. AA,AJ,1,T

9 Toshimaro Suso, 'A Proposal on an Accounting of Cost Variances in Standard Costing', *Sangyokeiri*, 1985, 1. AA,PJ,2,T

10 Takeo Yoshikawa, 'A Study and Analysis of Standard Variable Costing Systems', *Yokohama Business Review*, 1985, 3. AA,AJ,3,O

11 Shigeo Aoki, 'Factory Administration and Cost Accounting and Management Accounting', *Kigyokaikei*, 1985, 2. AA,CJ,3,T

12 Yutaka Kato, 'Management Accounting Practices of American Enterprises – A Survey for Applying Quantitative Decision Models', *Sangyokeiri*, 1985, 1. AA,PJ,6,T

13 Kengo Kogayashi, 'How Does Factory Administration Affect Budgeting and Standard Costing?', *Kigyokaikei*, 1985, 2. AA,CJ,2,T

14 Takao Makito, 'A Development of Factory Administration and the Way that Cost Management Should Be', *Kigyokaikei*, 1985, 2. AA,CJ,1,T

15 Sadao Mitsuoka, 'Opportunity Costs and Cost Accounting for Decision-making (1), (2)', *Konan Business Review*, 1984, 9. 1985, 1. AA,AJ,6,O

16 Michiharu Sakurai, 'FMS and New Developments in Management Accounting', *Kigyokaikei*, 1985, 2. AA,CJ,3,T

17 Fumio Yoshimura, 'Theoretical Evolution of Business Budgeting', *The Economic Review of Kanazawa University*, 1985, 1. AA,AJ,2,O

18 Hironori Ono, 'Class Cost System and Pricing Decision in the Country Elevation Management: An Examination of *Genkashugi* from the Viewpoint of *Jigyohoshiki*', *Journal of Rural Problems*, 1985, 3. AA,AJ,6,O

19 Yoshihiro Hirabayashi, 'Literatur der Kostenrechnung in Deutschland in 19 Jahrhundert' *['Literature about cost accounting in Nineteenth-century Germany']*, *Accounting*, 1985, 5. AA,AJ,4,O

20 Hiromasa Itani, 'Joint Cost Accounting Models by Linear Operation Factors', *Senshu Shogaku Ronshu*, 1985, 3. AA,AJ,1,T

21 Ichiei Kono, 'A Study on Cost Accounting', *Daitobunka University Kiyo Shakai Kagaku*, 1985, 3. AA,AJ,1,T

22 Mitsuro Kuno, 'Two Early Works on Cost Accounting in the United States – Works of H. Metcalfe and H.L. Arnold', *The Economic Review*, Otaru University of Commerce, 1985, 3. AA,AJ,4,T

23 Kaname Sakaguchi, 'Struktur und Funktionsweise der Betriebspankostenrechnung: Eine vergleichende Untersuchnung Zwischen Betriebspankostenrechnung und Grenzplankostenrechnung' *['The structure and function of internal budget costing: A comparative analysis of internal budget accounting and standard direct costing']*, *The Economics Society of Hiroshima University*, 1985, 3. AA,AJ,2,O

24 Akihiro Saki, 'Relative Variable Costing and Contribution Margin Calculation', *Wako Keizai*, 1985, 3. AA,AJ,1,T

25 Yoshitaka Sato, 'Relationship of Production-form and Costing-form', *Journal of Business and Economics*, Economics Society of Nagasaki University, 2. AA,AJ,1,O

26 Yoshikazu Toyoshima, 'Some Comments on the First Report of Nagasaki Arsenal in 1871–1877', *Annual Report of the Economic Society*, Tohoku University, 1985, 2. AA,AJ,4,O

27 Yoshitaka Hazama, 'Development of Welsch's Budgeting', *Quarterly Review*, Department of Economics, Nara Prefectural College, 1985, 1. AA,AJ,2,O

28 Tadashi Itagaki, 'The Mechanism of Budgetary Management and Management Accounting – One Approach to the Functions of Management Accounting', *Yamaguchi Journal of Economics, Business Administration and Laws*, 1985, 5. AA,AJ,2,O

29 Yutaka Kato, 'A Practical Use of Quantitative Approaches in Management Accounting – A Survey of Effectiveness Using Decision Support Systems', *Sangyokeiri*, 1985, 4. AA,PJ,6,T

30 Tsugio Kono, 'Die Funktionen des Managerial Accountings der Periodenbezogenen Kosten- und Erlosrechnung' *['The functions of managerial accounting in respect of period-related cost and revenue accounting']*, *Oita University Economic Review*, 1985, 1. AA,AJ,3,O

31 Ichiro Mizuno, 'A Generation of Added Value Management Accounting in Britain (1) – On the Added Value of F.R. Benley', *Keizaigaku-Ronshu of Kagoshima University*, 1985, 3. AA,AJ,3,O

32 Hiromitsu Sato, 'The Usefulness of Management Accounting Information under Multi-person Setting: Some Tests Based on Agency Model (4)', *The Waseda Journal of Social Sciences*, 1985, 3. AA,AJ,3,O

33 Yoshiho Tanaka, 'The Real State of Cost Control in Japan from 1955 to 1981', *The Kagawa University Economic Review*, 1985, 3. AA,AJ,2,O

34 Koji Yamamoto, 'The Usefulness of Management Accounting Information in the Decision Model Approach', *The Kagawa University Economic Review*, 1985, 3. AA,AJ,6,O

35 Hideo Yazawa, 'A Budgeting System for the Distribution Industries, Focusing on Welsch's Theory', *Kaikeigaku Kenkyu*,

Senshu University Kaikeigaku Kenkyujoyo, 1985, 3. AA,AJ,2,T

36 Manabu Sugiyama, 'Non-profit Organisations' Performance Evaluation', *Aoyama Journal of Business*, 1985, 3. AA,AJ,5,O

37 Hideyuki Imaki, 'Performance Evaluation and Conflict of a Multinational Enterprise', *St Andrews University Economic and Business Review*, 1985, 6. AA,AJ,5,O

38 Teruo Nakamura, 'Computer Accounting and Management Accounting Information', *Kigyokaikei*, 1985, 6. PA,CJ,3,T

39 Tatsuhiko Arakawa, 'Chushobumon and "Kumibetsu-Sogo" Cost System', *Meiji Accounting Review*, 1985, 3. AA,AJ,1,O

40 Toshiro Hiromoto, 'A Challenge Facing Cost Accounting in the Age of Innovation', *Accounting*, 1985, 7. AA,AJ,1,O

41 Yoshiro Ito, 'Cost Accounting with Micro RERO', *The Review of Takushoku University*, 1985, 5. AA,AJ,1,O

42 Sadao Kondo, 'Introduction to the History of Railway Cost Accounting Systems – Development of National Railway Cost Accounting Systems before the Second World War', *Business Studies Faculty of Business Administration*, 1985, 3. AA,AJ,4,O

43 Tsugio Kono, 'Die Preisuntergrenzenbestimmug und Direktkostenrechnung' *['Processing the lowest price limit and direct cost accounting'], Oita University Economic Review*, 1985, 7. AA,AJ,6,O

44 Masaaki Miyamoto, 'Production Process and Cost Accounting – A Study of Effective Factors in the Cost Accounting Process', *Kokumin Keizai Zasshi*, Kobe University, 1985, 9. AA,AJ,1,T

45 Naoki Murato, 'Cost Accounting in the Flexible Manufacturing System', *Journal of Liberal Arts and Economics*, Nagasaki Prefectural University of International Economics, 1985, 8. AA,AJ,1,O

46 Toshiharu Nakane, 'The Advanced Overhead Cost Distribution Method of William Sellers & Co. in the 1870s', *The Journal of Commerce and Economics, Meijo University*, 1985, 5. AA,AJ,4,O

47 Bunji Nishimura, 'A Study on a Stage of Completion of Conversion Cost for Process Costing', *Kigyokaikei*, 1985, 8. AA,CJ,1,T

48 Yoshitaka Sato, 'Character and Function of Production Orders in Cost Accounting', *Journal of Business and Economics, Nagasaki University*, 1985, 6. AA,AJ,1,O

49 Koichi Sumiya and Masahiko Yamamota, 'Introduction of Activity Costing', *Meiji Business Review*, 1985, 6. AA,AJ,1,O

50 Hiroaki Tatebe, 'The Historical Development of Cost Accounting', *Meiji Accounting Review*, 1985, 3. AA,AJ,4,O

51 Yoshikazu Toyoshima, 'Some Comments on Estimates of Building Expenses in the Tategami Plant, Nagasaki in 1878

(10)', *Annual Report of the Economic Society*, Tohoku University, 1985, 6. AA,AJ,4,O

52 Yoshikazu Toyoshima, 'Some Comments on Shipbuilding Records at Tategami Shipyard, Nagasaki Arsenal, in 1873', *Annual Report of the Economic Society*, Tohoku University, 1985, 9. AA,AJ,4,O

53 Kohei Yamada, 'The Development of Variable Costing', *Sangyokeiri*, 1985, 7. AA,PJ,1,T

54 Takayuki Asada, 'A Review of Management Accounting for Performance Evaluation – on the Issues of the Asymmetric Information in the Model of M.C. Penn and R.A. Dye', *Accounting*, 1985, 10. AA,AJ,3,O

55 Tamio Fushimi, 'DSS for Strategic Planning and Accounting Information', *Kigyokaikei*, 1985, 9. AA,CJ,6,T

56 Yukio Harada, 'Group Management and Management Accounting', *Sangyokeiri*, 1985, 7. AA,PJ,3,T

57 Yoshihiro Ito, 'Budgeting as a "Symbol" of Organisational Power Structures', *Journal of Economics*, Josai University, 1985, 7. AA,AJ,2,O

58 Yasuhiro Kadota, 'DSS for Management Accounting', *Kigyokaikei*, 1985, 9. AA,CJ,6,O

59 Yutaka Kato, 'Optimal Budgeting and DSS', *Kigyokaikei*, 1985, 9. AA,CJ,6,T

60 Toru Kishimoto, 'A Business Planning Simulation by DS-POESY', *Kigyokaikei*, 1985, 9. AA,CJ,6,T

61 Yoshio Matsushita, 'Total Profit Planning Systems by DSS', *Kigyokaikei*, 1985, 9. AA,CJ,6,T

62 Kazuo Nakajima, 'Model and Simulation by DSS Generator – Using IFPS', *Kigyokaikei*, 1985, 9. AA,CJ,6,T

63 Kiyoshi Okamoto, 'Control of Maintenance Costs in Japanese Factories', *Accounting*, 1985, 9. AA,AJ,1,T

64 Yoshiho Tanaka, 'The Real State of Cost Control in Japan from 1955 to 1981', *The Kanagawa University Economic Review*, 1985, 6. AA,AJ,4,O

65 Akira Toyama, 'DSS Practices for Management Accounting', *Kigyokaikei*, 1985, 9. AA,CJ,6,T

66 Tatsuto Yamagami, 'Accounting Information and Corporate Social Accounting', *Business Review*, Osaka City University, 1985, 7. AA,AJ,3,O

67 Fumio Yoshimura, 'Reconsideration on the Theoretical Framework of Management Accounting', *Economic Review*, Kanazawa University, 1985, 3. AA,AJ,3,O

68 Sadao Kondo, 'National Railway Cost Accounting System in the Transition Period to Public Corporation – A Note of the

Historical Studies on Railway Cost Accounting Systems', *The Journal of Commerce and Economics*, Meijo University, 1985, 5. AA,AJ,4,O

69 Takayuki Asada, 'The Performance Evaluation System for Searching Behaviour: Review on the Agency Model by Joseph Tzur', *St Andrews University Economic and Business Review*, 1985, 12. AA,AJ,5,O

70 Akira Ishikawa, 'Management Planning and Budgeting', *Nippon Keizai Kenkyu Center Kaiho*, 1985, 11. AA,AJ,2,T

71 Yoshiro Ito, 'The Process Costing by Micro REPO', Keiei Keiri Kenkyu, *Takushoku University*, 1985, 9. AA,AJ,1,T

72 Masashi Ryoto, 'Die Entwicklung der Direckt Kostenrechnung in Deutschland' *['The development of direct costing in Germany']*, *The Hikone Ronso*, Siga University, 1985, 11. AA,AJ,1,O

73 Kaname Sakaguchi, 'Der neueste Stand der Deutschen Kostenrechnungspaxis' *['The latest practice in German cost accounting']*, *The Hiroshima Economic Review*, 1985, 7. AA,AJ,1,O

74 Tadashi Shimura, 'On the Application of Cost Accounting in Non-profit Organisations', *The Review of Business Administration*, Soka University, 1985, 12. AA,AJ,1,O

75 Naohisa Sueishi, 'The Evolution and Direction of Cost Accounting – A Review of R.S. Kaplan's Article', *The Review of Osaka University of Commerce*, 1985, 6. AA,AJ,1,O

76 Yoshikazu Toyoshima, 'Some Comments on Specifications of Estimated Prices of Repairs on Ships at Nagasaki Dockyard and Engine Works in 1893', *Annual Report of the Economic Society*, 1985, 11. AA,AJ,4,O

77 Tamio Fushimi, 'The Concept of Strategic Management Accounting', *Kigyokaikei*, 1985, 12. AA,CJ,3,T

78 Yukio Harada, 'The Development of Strategic Budgeting', *Kigyokaikei*, 1985, 12. AA,CJ,2,T

79 Shuzo Iida, 'Added Value Accounting Information for Business Management', *Accounting*, 1985, 11. AA,AJ,9,O

80 Susumu Ito, 'Accounting Process for Profit Planning and Control', *Accounting*, 1985, 11. AA,AJ,2,O

81 Sadayoshi Maeda, 'Managerial Accounting and External Reporting', *The Journal of Musashi University*, 1985, 12. AA,AJ,3,O

82 Ichiro Mizuno, 'Extension in Accounting Information and Value Added Management Accounting', *Accounting*, 1985, 11. AA,AJ,3,O

83 Yasuhiro Monden, 'Management Accounting as Decision Support Systems', *Accounting*, 1985, 11. AA,AJ,6,O

84 Kiyoshi Ogawa, 'Extension of Accounting Information and Evaluation of Performance', *Accounting*, 1985, 11. AA,AJ,5,O

85 Kiyoshi Okamoto, 'An Extension of Management Accounting Standards – an Integration of Financial Management and Management Accounting', *Kigyokaikei*, 1986, 1. AA,CJ,8,T

86 6Koichi Saito, 'The Management Style and Responsibility Accounting at the Volvo Plant at Kalmar', *The Bulletin of the Graduate School of Commerce*, School of Social Sciences, Waseda University, 1985, 11. AA,AJ,2,O

87 Hiromitsu Sato, 'The Usefulness of Managerial Accounting Information under Multi-person Setting: Some Tests Based on Agency Model (5)', *The Waseda Journal of Social Sciences*, 1985, 10. AA,AJ,3,O

88 Satoru Yamada, 'Japanese Management and Performance Accounting', *The Bulletin of the Graduate School of Commerce*, Waseda University, 1985, 11. AA,AJ,5,O

89 Sadao Kondo, 'Discussion on the Economic Calculation System in JNR', *Komaza-Wa Business Review*, 1985, 6. AA,AJ,9,O

90 Bokuryo Nagahama, 'Performance Evaluation of International Operations', *Osaka Economic Papers*, 1985, 6. AA,AJ,5,O

91 Tetsuro Kobayashi, 'Absorption Costing and the Variation of Period Income', *The Journal of Economics, Hokkai-Gakuen University*, 1985, 12. AA,AJ,3,O

92 Masaaki Miyamoto, 'Cost Structure and Cost Accounting', *Osaka Economic Papers*, 1985, 6. AA,AJ,1,O

93 Sakurai Michiharo, 'Some of the Issues of Computer Software Accounting – A Study on Cost Accounting and its Property', *Senshu Keieigaku Ronshu*, 1985, 7. AA,AJ,1,T

94 Mikio Tokai, 'Costing and Profit Determination – A Review of the Period Cost Concept', *Aoyama Journal of Business*, 1985, 11. AA,AJ,3,O

95 Satoshi Wada, 'A Review of "Cost Accounting Standards"', *Quarterly Journal of Economics*, Kanto Gakuin University, 1985, 7. AA,AJ,8,O

96 Hidetoshi Ito, 'A Basic Study of Accounting for Social Responsibility: The State of Internal System of Accounting for Social Responsibility', *The Journal of Commerce and Economics*, Meijo University, 1985, 12. AA,AJ,3,O

97 Susumu Ito, 'Development of Segmental Management Accounting', *Papers of the Research Society, Hiroshima Shudo University*, 1985, 12. AA,AJ,5,O

98 Kazumasa Yoshida, 'A Study of Cost Accounting for Pricing', *Fuyama University Keizai Ronshu*, 1985, 12. AA,AJ,6,T

1986

1 Yukio Harada, 'Performance Evaluation and Improvement for a Group Management', *Sangyokeiri*, 1986, 1. AA,PJ,5,T
2 Hiromitsu Sato, 'The Usefulness of Managerial Accounting Information under Multi-person Setting: Some Tests Based on Agency Model (6)', *The Waseda Journal of Social Sciences*, 1986, 3. AA,AJ,3,O
3 Hiromasa Itani, 'EDV-oriented Managerial Economics and Cost Accounting', *Shogaku Kenkyu Nenpo*, Senshu University, 1986, 3. AA,AJ,1,T
4 Tsugio Kono, 'Eine Struktur einer kombineirten Grenzkosten – Vollkostenrechnung fur die Nachricht des Management Accounting' *['A structure combining direct costing and full costing for management accounting'], Oita University Economic Review*, 1986, 1. AA,AJ,1,O
5 Seiji Matsutani, 'Some Notes on Cost Developments in Britain and America in the Early Nineteenth Century', *Accounting*, 1986, 3. AA,AJ,4,O
6 Osamu Nishizawa, 'New Methods of Transportation Costing in the USA', *The Waseda Commercial Review*, 1986, 2. AA,AJ,1,O
7 Ryoten Shirakawa, 'Cost Accounting for Software', *Kenkyu Nenpo*, Nihon University, 1986, 2. AA,AJ,1,T
8 Mikio Tokai, 'A Study on Interlinking Costing with Profit Determination', *Accounting*, 1986, 2. AA,AJ,1,O
9 Yukio Harada, 'Strategic Planning and Budgeting', *Zeimutsushin*, 1986, 3. AA,CJ,2,T
10 Taisaku Takei, 'A Study on Decentralisation for Strategic Planning', *Kigyokaikei*, 1986, 6. AA,CJ,6,T
11 Toshio Kida, 'Origin of Cost Management and Break-even Chart by Hess', *Osaka Gakuin University Shokei Ronso*, 1986, 1. AA,AJ,4,T
12 Hiromasa Itani, 'Fixed Cost Issues and a Partial Cost Accounting', *Kaikeigaku Kenkyu*, Senshu University, 1986, 3. AA,AJ,1,T
13 Yoshiro Ito, 'The Process Costing by Micro REPO', *Keiei Keiri Kenkyu*, Takushoku University, 1986, 2. AA,AJ,1,T
14 Sadao Kondo, 'Accounting Revolution? Accounting System of the JNR during the Period of High Economic Growth in Japan', *Komazawa Business Review*, 1986, 2. AA,AJ,4,O
15 Chikayoshi Kurata, 'Profit Planning and Variable Costing', *Sappro Gakuin Shokei Ronshu*, 1986, 3. AA,AJ,6,T
16 Seiji Matsutani, 'British and American Cost Accounting from the Early to the Mid-nineteenth Century', *Accounting*, 1986, 4. AA,AJ,4,T

17 Masaaki Miyamoto, 'Issues and Review of Modern Cost Accounting', *Kigyokaikei*, 1986, 7. AA,CJ,1,T
18 Michiharu Sakurai, 'A Mechanism of Cost Accounting for Software', *Sangyokeiri*, 1986, 4. AA,PJ,1,T
19 Kazuo Arai, 'A Participative Type of Budgeting, Locus of Control and Leadership Style', *Bunkei Ronso*, Hirosaki University, 1986, 3. AA,AJ,2,T
20 Tamio Fushimi, 'A Strategic-oriented Budgeting and Accounting System', *Kigyokaikei*, 1986, 6. AA,CJ,2,T
21 Iwao Futami, 'A Development of Contingency Plans for Budgeting Systems', *The Accounting Research*, 1986, 4. AA,AJ,2,T
22 Toshiro Hiromoto, 'Some Observations on Management Accounting in Japanese Manufacturing Companies', *Business Review*, Hitotsubashi University, 1986, 3. AA,AJ,7,O
23 Yutaka Kato, 'Empirical Research on the Current Management Accounting Practice in Large American Corporations – Re-evaluation of the User Decision – Model Approach', *Accounting*, 1986, 6. AA,AJ,7,O
24 Akira Kawai, 'The Necessity to Re-examine Management Accounting Systems', *Kigyokaikei*, 1986, 6. AA,CJ,3,T
25 Masaaki Miyamoto, 'Cost Accounting and Cost Theory', *Business Review*, Osaka University, 1986, 3. AA,AJ,1,O
26 Teruo Nakamura, 'Decision-making and Support Systems', *Business Review*, Osaka University, 1986, 3. AA,AJ,6,O
27 Osamu Nishizawa, 'Management of R. & D. Expenses in the Hi-Tech Age', *Kigyokaikei*, 1986, 6. AA,CJ,1,T
28 Kiyoshi Okamoto, 'History of Cost Accounting and Management Accounting in Hitotsubashi University', *Hitotsubashi Ronso*, 1986, 4. AA,AJ,4,T
29 Kiyoshi Okamoto, 'Interaction of Management Accounting and Financial Management', *Business Review*, Hitotsubashi University, 1986, 3. AA,AJ,3,O
30 Hiroyuki Itami and Syotaro Watanabe, 'Strategies and Management Accounting', *Kigyokaikei*, 1986, 6. AA,CJ,3,T
31 Takeyuki Tani, 'Management Accounting Systems in the Changing Organisational Environment', *Business Review*, Kobe University, 1986, 3. AA,AJ,3,O
32 Kanji Miyamoto, 'Accounting Issues of Performance Evaluation of Overseas Junior Companies – Focusing on Accounting for Foreign Current Exchange and Price Changes', *Kigyokaikei*, 1986, 9. AA,CJ,5,T
33 Genri Hisatomi, 'Zur Grundlkonzeption der Einzelkostenrechnung' *['On the basic concept of direct costing']*, *Kobe-Gakuin Economic Papers*, 1986, 6. AA,AJ,1,O

34 Junko Odagiri, 'Zu den Auswirkungen der Besteuerung auf die Kostenrechnung' *['Effects of taxation on cost accounting'], The Hikone Ronso*, Shiga University, 1986, 1. AA,AJ,1,O

35 Masaaki Ryoto, 'Direct Costing Systems in West Germany', *Accounting*, 1986, 9. AA,AJ,1,O

36 Isao Iizuka, 'Measurement and Communication in Management Accounting', *Accounting*, 1986, 9. AA,AJ,3,O

37 Jinji Oshikawa and Robert S. Kaplan, 'Advanced Management Accounting (1)', *Business Review*, Osaka City University, 1986, 7. AA,AJ,3,O

38 Susumu Ito, 'The Functions of Management Accounting – Contribution to Corporate Organisational Behaviour', *Kigyokaikei*, 1986, 8. AA,CJ,3,T

39 Yutaka Kato, 'Management Accounting Practices of Japanese Companies – Survey of Application of Quantitative Decision-making Models', *Sangyokeiri*, 1986, 10 AA,CJ,6,T

40 Takao Makito, 'Life Cycle Costing and Cost Management', *Accounting*, 1986, 9. AA,AJ,1,O

41 Shunzo Matsuoka, 'Managerial Cost Incurrence and Responsibility Accounting', *Bulletin of Hannan University*, 1986, 3. AA,AJ,2,O

42 Hideshi Nagamatsu, 'An Introduction to Cost Control on Flexible Manufacturing Systems', *Komazawa Business Review*, 1986, 3. AA,AJ,2,O

43 Michiharu Sakurai, 'Cost Management of Software', *Sangyokeiri*, 1986, 7. AA,PJ,1,T

44 Yasuo Sato, 'Re-examination of Management Accounting under Factory Automation and Flexible Manufacturing Systems (1)', *The Hosei Journal of Business*, 1986, 7. AA,AJ,3,O

45 Shigeo Aoki, 'Development of Japanese Cost Accounting – A Study of the Literature between the Early Taisho Era and World War II', *Kaikeigaku Kenkyu*, Nihon University, 1986, 12. AA,AJ,4,T

46 Toshiyasu Kato, 'Costing for Inventory Valuation', T*he Economic Review of Komazawa University*, 1986, 11. AA,AJ,1,O

47 Toshiharu Nakane, 'Scientific Management and Cost Accounting at Watertown Arsenal', *The Journal of Commerce and Economics*, Meijo University, 1986, 6. AA,AJ,4,O

48 Hiroshi Torii, 'Process-Cost Accounting Procedures and Waste', *The Papers and Proceedings of Economics*, Meiji-Gakuin, 1986, 12. AA,AJ,1,O

49 Tamio Fushimi, 'Strategic Management Accounting and Cash Flow Information: In View of Decisionalised Management Control', *Accounting*, 1986, 12. AA,AJ,3,O

50 Susumu Ito, 'Development of Segment Management Accounting', *Accounting*, 1986, 12. AA,AJ,5,O

51 Yoshihiro Ito, '"Direct Research" in the Field of Management Accounting', *Journal of Economics*, Josai University, 1986, 12. AA,AJ,3,O

52 Kengo Kobayashi, 'The Beginning of Business Organisation Theory and Its Emphasis on Accounting Procedures – The Background of the Evolution of Business Budgeting', *Aoyama Journal of Business*, 1986, 11. AA,AJ,2,O

53 Kengo Kobayashi, 'On the Origins of Business Budgeting – The First Chapter in the Evolution of Business Budgeting', *Aoyama Journal of Business*, 1986, 11. AA,AJ,4,O

54 Tetsuo Kobayashi, 'Management Accounting in Divisionalised Organisations: Allocation of Corporate Costs', *Accounting*, 1986, 12. AA,AJ,1,O

55 Yasumasa Kondo, 'A Survey of Consciousness of Management Accounting by the Controllers', *The Doshisha Business Review*, 1986, 6. AA,AJ,7,T

56 Naoki Murata, 'Just-in-Time and Management Accounting', *Journal of Liberal Arts and Economics*, Nagasaki Prefectural University, 1986, 12. AA,AJ,3,O

57 Michiharu Sakuari, 'Research Methodologies of Management Accounting in a Changing Environment', *Accounting*, 1986, 12. AA,AJ,3,O

58 Hiromitsu Sato, 'The Usefulness of Managerial Accounting Information under Multi-person Setting: Some Tests Based on Agency Model (7), (8)', *Waseda Journal of Social Sciences*, 1986, 10. 1987, 3. AA,AJ,3,O

59 Yasuo Sato, 'Re-examination of Management Accounting under FA and FMS (II)', *The Hosei Journal of Business*, 1986, 10 AA,AJ,3,O

60 Yoshiho Tanaka, 'The Real State of Cost Control in Japan from 1955 to 1981 (3)', *The Kagawa University Economic Review*, 1986, 12. AA,AJ,4,O

61 Yoshitaka Hazama, 'On Bromwich's Economics of Capital Budgeting', *Kenkyu Kiho*, Nara Prefectural Junior University, 1986, 12. AA,AJ,2,O

62 Takeaki Okamoto, 'Divisional Organisation and Performance Evaluation', *Kenkyu Kiyo*, Aomori University, 1986, 10. AA,AJ,5,T

63 Manami Motohashi, 'On F.W. Taylor's Cost Accounting System', *Meiji Business Review*, 1986, 12. AA,AJ,4,O

64 Susumu Ito, 'Current Issues of Management Accounting for Common Cost – Segment Accounting for Common Cost', *Shudo*

Shogaku, Hiroshima University, 1986, 8. AA,AJ,1,T
65 Masaaki Miyamoto, 'CIM and Cost Accounting Systems', *Osaka Economic Papers*, 1986, 9. AA,AJ,1,O
66 Bokuryo Nagahama, 'About "The Evolution of Management Accounting"', *Osaka Economic Papers*, 1986, 9. AA,AJ,4,O
67 Shokichi Nakahara, 'Added Value Management Accounting Data in Hospitals', *The Economic Review of Komazawa University*, 1986, 12. AA,AJ,3,O
68 Yoshikazu Sunada, 'A Study of Corporate Performance – Electric and Electronics Equipment Corporations in Japan (1), (2)', *The Soka Economic Studies Quarterly*, 1986, 3. AA,AJ,5,O

1987

1 Yoshihiro Hirabayashi, 'Some Problems with Cost Accounting Standards', *Journal of Business Administration of Kwansai Gakuen University*, 1987, 3. AA,AJ,8,O
2 Johokashakai to Genkakeisan Iinkai, 'Some of the Issues Relating to Factory Automation', *Kigyokaikei*, 1987, 4. AA,CJ,3,T
3 Johokashakai to Genkakeisan Iinkai, 'Cost Accounting for Service', *Kigyokaikei*, 1987, 4. AA,CJ,1,T
4 Johokassakai to Genkakeisan Iinkai, 'Character and Mechanism of Cost Accounting for Software', *Kigyokaikei*, 1987, 4. AA,CJ,1,T
5 Yoshitaka Kijima, 'Cost Accounting with the Fourth Cost Factor and its Benefit', *Shogaku Hensan*, Chuo University, 1987, 1. AA,AJ,1,T
6 Yoshitaka Kijima, 'Factory Automation and Costs', *Kigyokaikei*, 1987, 4. AA,CJ,1,T
7 Yasuo Sato, 'Adequacy of Cost Accounting Systems: Based on a Comparison Between Japan and America', *The Hosei Journal of Business*, 1987, 1. AA,AJ,1,O
8 Tadashi Shimura, 'Soft Economy and Cost Accounting', *Kigyokaikei*, 1987, 4. AA,CJ,1,T
9 Tohei Uchiyama, 'Fundamental Framework of Cost Accounting for Software', *Kigyokaikei*, 1987, 4. AA,CJ,1,T
10 Hitoshi Yanagida, 'Die Entwicklung von Kostenrechnung zur Management Accounting – Aufgaben der Kostenrechnung als bestimmende Elemente die Gestaltung von Kostenrechnungssysytemen' *['The evolution of cost accounting to management accounting - the functions of cost accounting as a determining element in designing costing systems']*, *The Nagoya University Review*, 1987, 1. AA,AJ,1,O
11 Takeo Yoshikawa, 'Job Costing for Software Development', *Kigyokaikei*, 1987, 4. AA,CJ,1,O

12 Shinichi Inoue, 'A Survey of Cost Management Systems in Japanese Manufacturing Companies', *The Kagawa University Economic Review*, 1987, 3. AA,AJ,1,O

13 Yutaka Kato, 'Management Accounting Practices of Japanese Companies – A Survey of the Application of Quantitative Decision-making Models', *Sangyokeiri*, 1987, 1. AA,PJ,6,T

14 Masanobu Kosuga, 'Conceptual Framework for Management Accounting Research', *Journal of Business Administration*, Kwansei Gakuin University, 1987, 3. AA,AJ,2,O

15 Masanobu Kosuga, 'The Information Bias in Budgeting', *Journal of Business Administration*, Kwansei Gakuin University, 1987, 3. AA,AJ,2,O

16 Yoshihiro Naka, 'On Budgetary Slack', *The Economic Review*, Oyaru University of Commerce, 1987, 1. AA,AJ,2,O

17 Michiharu Sakurai, 'Advanced Information Society and the Change of Corporate Management', *Kigyokaikei*, 1987, 4. AA,AJ,9,T

18 Seiichi Sato, 'Management Accounting in the Changing Environment', *Accounting*, 1987, 2. AA,AJ,3,O

19 Seiichi Sato, 'A Change of Manufacturing Environment and Management Accounting', *Kigyokaikei*, 1987, 4. AA,CJ,3,T

20 Fumiyasu Takahashi, 'A Change in Cost Management', *Kigyokaikei*, 1987, 4. AA,CJ,1,T

21 Michio Nakamura, 'Development of Main Figures and Indexes for Evaluating Achievement of Factories and Combines in the GDR', *The Bulletin of the Faculty of Commerce*, Meiji University, 1987. AA,AJ,5,O

22 Shinichi Korogi, 'Review of Thomas Johnson's Paper – New Understanding of Nineteenth-century Cost Accounting', *Kyushu Kyoritsu University Kiyo*, 1987, 3. AA,AJ,4,T

23 Yoshihiro Hirabayashi, 'Innovation and Cost Accounting', *Accounting*, 1987, 5. AA,AJ,1,O

24 Akira Ibushi, 'Investitinsrechnung ung Kostenrechnung' *['Investment appraisal and cost accounting']*, *The Annual Review of Economics, Business and Law*, 1987, 3. AA,AJ,1,O

25 Tsugio Kono, 'Seichts Stufenwise Grenzkostenrechnung und seine Denkweise der Abbauf Higkeit – Ein Beitrag zur Weiterentwicklung der Deckungsbeitragsrechnung' *['The nature of gradual direct costing – A contribution to the further development of marginal costing']*, *Oita University Economic Review*, 1987, 1. AA,AJ,1,O

26 Masaaki Miyamoto, 'On the New Cost Accounting System', *Accounting*, 1987, 5. AA,AJ,1,O

27 Junko Odagiri, 'Cost Accounting for a Commerce Business',

Hikone Ronso, 1987, 1. AA,AJ,1,T
28 Kenji Okano, 'An Application of Variable Costing to Job Costing', *Matsuyama Shodai Ronso*, 1987, 2. AA,AJ,1,T
29 Teruo Okamura, 'A Study of Depreciation for Cost Accounting – Review of the paper by W. Marhlberg', *Shogaku Kenkyu Nenpo*, Senshu University, 1987. AA,AJ,1,T
30 Kazuo Osawa, 'A Study of Fixed Costs in Relevant Costing', *Meiji Accounting Review*, 1987, 3. AA,AJ,1,O
31 Kiyoshi Sakamoto, 'Cost Accounting Issues and New Trends for the Reform Age', *Meidai Shogaku Ronso*, Meiji University, 1987, 2. AA,AJ,1,T
32 Hiroaki Tatebe, 'Uber die Zusammenhang zwischen Finanzbuchhaltung und Kostenrechnung' *['Similarities between financial accounting and cost accounting']*, *Meiji Accounting Review*, 1987, 3. AA,AJ,1,O
33 Kazuo Aida, 'Budgeting for Non-profit Organisations', *Dokkyo University Keizaigaku Kenkyu*, 1987, 1. AA,AJ,2,T
34 Hiroshi Ito, 'Budgeting in the Business Strategy Age', *Kigyokaikei*, 1987, 7. AA,CJ,2,T
35 Yoshihiro Ito, 'A Critical Analysis of Descriptive Researches on Budgeting', *Kigyokaikei*, 1987, 7. AA,CJ,2,T
36 Shuzo Kamijo, 'New Viewpoints of Budgeting', *Kigyokaikei*, 1987, 7. AA,CJ,2,T
37 Shuzo Kamijo, 'The Possibility of a Contingency Approach for Management Accounting and its Problems', *Tokyo Toritsu Shoka Tanki University Kenkyu Ronso*, 1987, 2. AA,AJ,3,T
38 Akira Kaneko, 'Think of Modern Budgeting', *Kigyokaikei*, 1987, 7. AA,CJ,2,T
39 Toru Katori, 'The Effects of Inflation for the Accounting Management: Introduction', *The Research Bulletin of Kanto Gakuen University*, 1987, 2. AA,AJ,3,O
40 Kengo Kobayashi, 'The Development of Functional Decentralisation and the Co-ordination of Functions – The Background of the Evolution of Business Budgeting', *Aoyama Journal of Business*, 1987, 3. AA,AJ,2,O
41 Yasumasa Kondo, 'Development of Budgeting Based on Contingency Theory', *Kigyokaikei*, 1987, 7. AA,CJ,2,T
42 Hideshi Nagamatsu, 'Some Issues of Performance Evaluation', Business Studies, *Komazawa University*, 1987, 3. AA,AJ,5,O
43 Akira Nishimura, 'Development of Management Accounting Research', *Keizaigaku Kenkyu*, Kyushu University, 1987, 2. AA,AJ,3,T
44 Noboru Ogura, 'Organisational Hierarchy and Management Accounting for Performance Evaluation', *Kenkyu Nenpo*

Keizaigaku, 1987, 3. AA,AJ,5,T

45 Masao Sato, 'A Locus of Cost Management in Japan – A Review of Professor Imai's Theory', *Sangyokeiri*, 1987, 4. AA,PJ,1,T

46 Masao Tsuji, 'Budgeting System by DSS', *Kigyokaikei*, 1987, 7. AA,CJ,2,T

47 Hiromitsu Sato, 'The Profit Concept for Performance Evaluation', *Kigyokaikei*, 1987, 8. AA,CJ,5,T

48 Yutaka Kato, 'Performance Evaluation and Profit Information', *Kigyokaikei*, 1987, 8. AA,CJ,5,T

49 Jiro Asaba, 'Logic of the Formative Process of Cost Accounting Systems in Germany', *Accounting*, 1987, 8. AA,AJ,1,O

50 Masaaki Miyamoto, 'Idle Capacity Cost and Cost Accounting', *Sangyokeiri*, 1987, 7. AA,PJ,1,T

51 Hiroshi Okano, 'History of Cost Accounting by Murray C. Wells: A Review Essay', *Business Review*, Osaka City University, 1987, 8. AA,AJ,4,O

52 Hiroshi Okano and M.C. Wells, 'Historical Meaning of Cost Accounting History by M.C. Wells', *Osaka Ichidai Roinshu*, 1987, 6. AA,AJ,4,T

53 Michiharu Sakurai, 'The Realities of Cost Accounting for Software', *Kigyokaikei*, 1987, 9. AA,CJ,1,T

54 Toshikazu Toyoshima, 'Case Study of Cost Accounting at the Mitsubishi Shipping Company in the Meiji and Taisho Eras', *Kenkyu Nenpo Keizaigaku*, Tokyo University, 1987, 5. AA,AJ,1.T

55 Junji Ishikawa and Robert S. Kaplan, 'Advanced Management Accounting (2)', *The Keiei Kenkyu*, Osaka City University, 1987, 6. AA,AJ,3,O

56 Yasumasa Kondo, 'A Survey of Consciousness of Management Accounting System by Heads of Divisions', *Doshisha Shogaku*, 1987, 7. AA,AJ,7,T

57 Yasuo Sato, 'Factory Automation and Management Accounting – Some of the Issues in Japanese Companies', *The Hosei Journal of Business*, 1987, 7. AA,AJ,3,T

1988

1 Yasumasa Kondo, 'Some Observations on Management Accounting Practice in Japanese Manufacturing Companies', *The Doshisha Business Review*, 1988, 7. AA,AJ,3,O

2 Yasumasa Kondo, 'Some Observations on Management Accounting Practice in Japanese Manufacturing Companies', *The Doshisha Business Review*, 1988, 8. AA,AJ,3,O

3 Kazumasa Nakada, 'Decision Support Systems and Budgeting Systems', *Aizu Junior College*, 1988, 3. AA,AJ,6,T

4 Shuji Okuyama, 'The Paradox of Responsibility Accounting

and the Relative Responsibility Accounting's Function', *The Shogaku Ronso*, The Economic Society of Fukushima University, 1988, 3. AA,AJ,2,O

5 Koji Miyoshi, 'A Historical Study of the Evolution of Budgeting Control in the USA', *The Shogaku Ronso*, The Economic Society of Fukushima University, 1988, 3. AA,AJ,4,O

6 Koji Miyoshi, 'A View of Horngren's Theory of Management Science', *The Shogaku Ronso*, The Economic Society of Fukushima University, 1988, 8. AA,AJ,3,O

7 Kazuo Amai, 'A Study on Contribution Margin of Variable Costing', *The Business Review of Kansai University*, 1988, 12. AA,AJ,1,O

8 Fumio Sakai, 'On the Relationship Between Cost and Expense', *The Business Review of Kansai University*, 1988, 12. AA,AJ,1,O

9 Takanori Furuta, 'A Management Accounting Approach to Inflation Accounting based on Edward Bell's Proposal', *Shogaku Ronshu*, Osaka Gakuin University, 1988, 4. AA,AJ,3,T

10 Toshio Honda, 'The Germination of Standard Costing in the US Shoe Industry: A Review of F.L. Small's Opinions', *Osaka Gakuin Business Review*, 1988, 12. AA,AJ,4,T

11 Hideshi Nagamatsu, 'Some Reviews of Cost Accounting in the New Manufacturing Environment', *Accounting*, 1988, 3. AA,AJ,1,O

12 Yoshitake Heshiki, 'Relation Between Principles of Recognisation on the Cost and Lower of Cost or Market', *Accounting*, 1988, 3. AA,AJ,1,O

13 Takayuki Asada, 'Empirical Study of Participative Budgeting, Performance Measurement and Evaluation', *Accounting*, 1988, 8. AA,AJ,2,O

14 Yoshikazu Toyoshima, 'Reconsideration of an Application of Kuhn's Paradigm to Management Accounting', *Accounting*, 1988, 9. AA,AJ,3,O

15 Mikio Tokai, 'A Suggestion on Getting Out of Some Ideas Underlying Traditional Cost Accounting', *Accounting*, 1988, 9. AA,AJ,1,O

16 Shuji Mizoguchi, 'A View of Managerial Accounting Systems Applied to Structural Change of Organisations', *Accounting*, 1988, 11. AA,AJ,3,O

17 Hiroshi Sakane, 'Joint Cost Allocation and Product Costing', *Accounting*, 1988, 11. AA,AJ,1,O

18 Takeyuki Tani, 'Allocation of Corporate Costs for Performance Control', *Accounting*, 1988, 12. AA,AJ,5,O

19 Hiroshi Ito, 'Introduction of "Re-Usefulness"', *Kigyokaikei*, 1988, 2. AA,CJ,9,T

20 Tetsu Kobayashi, 'Business Strategies and Management Accounting Systems', *Kigyokaikei*, 1988, 4. AA,CJ,3,T
21 Norio Shibata, 'Budgeting Systems of Japanese Companies (1)', *Kigyokaikei*, 1988, 4. AA,CJ,2,T
22 Masaaki Miyamoto, 'Technological Innovation and Cost Management', *Kigyokaikei*, 1988, 5. AA,CJ,1,T
23 Michiharu Sakurai, 'Significance Target Costing in a High-Tech Environment', *Kigyokaikei*, 1988, 5. AA,CJ,1,T
24 Yasuhiro Monden, 'JIT and Costing/Cost Management – A Case Study of Daihatsu Industry', *Kigyokaikei*, 1988, 5. AA,CJ,1,T
25 Norio Shibata, 'Budgeting Systems of Japanese Companies (2)', *Kigyokaikei*, 1988, 6. AA,CJ,2,T
26 Akira Yoshida, 'A Management Accounting Approach to Business Strategies of International Companies', *Kigyokaikei*, 1988, 9. AA,CJ,3,T
27 Osamu Nishizawa, 'A Practical Example of Introducing a Strategic Independent Profit System', *Kigyokaikei*, 1988, 9. AA,CJ,6,T
28 Muneya Sato, 'Developing an Accounting Information Network – A Practical Example', *Kigyokaikei*, 1988, 9. AA,CJ,3,T
29 Tohei Uchiyama, 'Some Problems of Management Accounting in the Information Society', *Kigyokaikei*, 1988, 9. AA,CJ,3,T
30 Yasuo Sato, 'Automatic Production System and Cost Accounting: Based on the Symposium of the NAA and AAA', *Kigyokaikei*, 1988, 9. AA,CJ,1,T
31 Masanobu Kogure, 'Relevance Lost in the Study of Budgeting', *Kigyokaikei*, 1988, 9. AA,CJ,2,T
32 Kiyoshi Ogawa, 'Delegation of Power in a Decentralised Organisation and Accounting Systems', *Kigyokaikei*, 1988, 11. AA,CJ,5,T
33 Seiji Mastutani, 'Development of the Standard Costing Way of Thinking in the UK', *Kigyokaikei*, 1988, 11. AA,CJ,4,T
34 Yasuo Sato, 'Industry/University Co-operation for Restructuring of Management Accounting', *Sangyokeiri*, 1988, 1. AA,PJ,3,T
35 Noboru Ogara, 'Non-Atomic Game and Standard Costing', *Sangyokeiri*, 1988, 4. AA,PJ,2,T
36 Hiroshi Torii, 'A Possibility of Offering Profit Incentive to Cost Centres', *Sangyokeiri*, 1988, 4. AA,PJ,5,T
37 Masaaki Imabayashi, 'A Study of Transfer Pricing by Turning Service Centres into Profit Centres', *Sangyokeiri*, 1988, 4. AA,PJ,5,T
38 Hideshi Nagamatsu, 'A Theme of Factory Automation and Cost Accounting – Measurement of Information System Cost and its

Accounting', *Sangyokeiri*, 1988, 7. AA,PJ,1,T
39 Yoshizumi Ohtaka, 'The Trend of Accounting Studies in China', *Sangyokeiri*, 1988, 7. AA,PJ,7,T
40 Yoichi Kataoka, 'CVP Analysis of a Local Power Plant Project', *Sangyokeiri*, 1988, 7. AA,PJ,6,T
41 Suguru Nakagawa, 'An Application of DSS to Management Accounting, Focusing on to Capital Budgeting', *Rokkodai Ronshu*, Kobe University, 1988, 7. AA,AJ,6,T
42 Sadao Mitsuoka, 'Cost Accounting at the Turn of the Century in Britain and the USA (1)', *Konan Business Review*, Konan University, 1988, 9. AA,AJ,4,O
43 Sadao Mitsuoka, 'Cost Accounting at the Turn of the Century in Britain and the USA (2)', *Konan Business Review*, Konan University, 1988, 11. AA,AJ,4,O
44 Hiroshi Sakane, 'Overhead Costing and Profit Management in Product Costing', *The Shodai Ronshu*, Kobe University of Commerce, 1988, 3. AA,AJ,1,T
45 Sadao Takatera, 'Accounting for Organisational Democracy: Towards a Genuine "Control With" Sub-units', *The Economic Review*, Kyoto University, 1988, 4/5. AA,AJ,2,O
46 Ryoji Abe, 'A Theme of Management Accounting in Agricultural Industries', *Nogyo Keisangaku Kenkyu*, Kyoto University, 1988, 12. AA,AJ,3,T
47 Kenji Okano, 'A Study of Horngren's Management Accounting – Relationships Between Accounting Systems and Management Processes', *The Matsuyamashodai Ronshu*, 1988, 8. AA,AJ,3,T
48 Kenji Okano, 'A Study of Horngren's Management Accounting – Design of Management Control Systems', *The Matsuyama-shodai Ronshu*, 1988, 10. AA,AJ,2,T
49 Mitsumasa Naka, 'Logistics Costs Management by Standard Costing and Flexible Budgeting', *Asahi Business Review*, Asahi University, 1988, 12. AA,AJ,2,O
50 Yoshinori Shirakawa, 'Accounting Analysis of Software', *Annual Study Report*, Nippon University, 1988, 2. AA,AJ,9,T
51 Fumiyasu Takahashi, 'The Structures and Themes of Cost Accounting in Japan', *Studies of Accounting*, Nippon University, 1988. AA,AJ,1,T
52 Hajime Yasukuni, 'Cost and Managerial Accounting Practices Australia Companies', *Asia University Management Review*, 1988, 10 AA,AJ,7,O
53 Yoshitake Heshiki, 'The Essentials of "Lower of Cost and Market"', *The Journal of Economic Studies*, University of Osaka Prefecture, 1988, 9. AA,AJ,1,O
54 Kaname Sakaguchi, 'Grundstruktur der Periodenerfolgs-

rechnungsmodelle' *['Basic structure of the profit and loss calculation model']*, *The Hiroshima Economic Review*, Hiroshima University, 1988, 6. AA,AJ,5,O

55 Yoshitaka Hazama, 'Uber Selbstkostenrechnung und Preispolitik von E. Schmalenbach (1)' *['A case study of the cost calculation and pricing policy of a German Company']*, *Quarterly Review*, Nara Prefectural College, 1988, 8. AA,AJ,6,O

56 Ysuyoshi Matsumoto, 'Die Rechnungsorganisation von R. Lowenstein' *['The organisation of accounts in the calculation of profitability']*, *Osaka Keidai Ronshu*, 1988, 3. AA,AJ,5,O

57 Toshihiko Kojima, 'Changes in Production Structures and Management Accounting', *Sangyo-Noritsu*, 1988, 10. AA,AJ,3,T

58 Syunzo Matsuoka, 'A Problem of Cost Allocation in Direct Costing', *Bulletin of Hannan University*, Social Science, 1988, 9. AA,AJ,1,O

59 Hiroshi Okano, 'History of Cost Accounting by Murray C. Wells: A Review Essay (2)', *Business Review*, Osaka City University, 1988, 10. AA,AJ,4,O

60 Fujio Aida, 'The Substance of Class Cost Systems', *Kitami Daigakuronshu*, 1988, 3. AA,AJ,1,T

61 Yoshihiro Naka, 'Corporate Competitive Strategies and Management Accounting Systems', *The Economic Review*, Otaru University of Commerce, 1988, 3. AA,AJ,3,O

62 Yoshiharu Fukushima, 'The Dawning of Cost Accounting', *The Economic Review*, Otaru University of Commerce, 1988, 3. AA,AJ,4,O

63 Noboru Harada, 'The Role of Post-decision Information in the Performance Evaluation', *Sapporo Gakuin University Review of Economics and Business*, 1988, 8. AA,AJ,5,O

64 Makoto Yori, 'Controllability and the Theory of Responsibility – Cost Allocation Based on Power Bases', *The Journal of Ryutsu Keizai University*, 1988, 10. AA,AJ,1,O

65 Hiromasa Itani, 'Eines Betriebliche Strukturmodell und Kostenstrukturanalysen' *['A business model and the analysis of cost structure']*, *The Kaikengaku Kenkyu*, Senshu University, 1988, 3. AA,AJ,1,O

66 Takeo Shibuya, 'Early Management Accounting at E.I. duPont de Nemours Powder Company', *The Kaikengaku Kenkyu*, Senshu University, 1988, 3. AA,AJ,4,O

67 Satoshi Yoshimura, 'On the Direct Costing Controversy', *Meiji Business Review*, Meiji University, 1988, 10. AA,AJ,1,O

68 Satoshi Yoshimura, 'On the Evolution of Direct Costing', *Memoir of the Graduate School*, Meiji University, 1988, 2. AA,AJ,4,O

69 Junzo Wada, 'The Complexity of Budgeting and Cost Management', *Study Report*, Okayama University, 1988, 5.A,AJ,2,O
70 Seiichi Shimizu, 'Useful Management Cost Accounting – A View of Management Cost Accounting for the 90s', *The Review of the Osaka University of Commerce*, 1988, 10. AA,AJ,3,O
71 Naohisa Sueishi, 'The Direction of Management Accounting – Porter and Akers's Criticism of Johnson and Kaplan's View', *The Review of the Osaka University of Commerce*, 1988, 10. AA,AJ,3,O
72 Yoshiaki Shoda, 'Computers for College Accounting Education', *Bulletin of the Institute for the Study of Economics*, Tokuyama University, 1988, 3. AA,AJ,9,O
73 Toshiyasu Kato, 'A Review of the Relevance Lost Concept', *The Economic Review of Komazawa University*, 1988, 2. AA,AJ,3,O
74 Haruo Hisamatsu, 'A Study on the Factory Overhead', *Business Studies, Faculty of Business Administration*, Komazawa University, 1988, 3. AA,AJ,1,O
75 Masao Ueno, 'Profit Planning and C-V-P Analysis in Management Accounting', *The Bulletin of the Faculty of Economics*, Wako University, 1988, 2. AA,AJ,6,O
76 Masao Ueno, 'The Evolution of Management Accounting', *The Bulletin of the Faculty of Economics*, Wako University, 1988, 3. AA,AJ,3,O
77 Hiroshi Narita, 'Intervention of an Arbitrary in Common Cost Allocation', *Accounting Research*, 1988, 10. AA,AJ,1,T
78 Koichi Sumiya, 'A History of Standard Costing, Focusing on its Age of Establishment', *Social Science Study Review*, Meiji University, 1988, 3. AA,AJ,4,T
79 Tadakazu Nakase, '"Mandatory" Accounting, "Voluntary" Accounting, and "Financial Accounting"', *The Journal of Commerce*, Chuo University, 1988, 2. AA,AJ,9,O
80 Yoshitaka Kijima, 'On the Recent Studies of Quality Costs in America', *The Journal of Commerce*, Chuo University, 1988, 3. AA,AJ,1,O
81 Hidero Tsuru, 'Decision-making Under Uncertainty in Cost Accounting', *Review of the Economic Society*, Sapporo University, 1988, 9. AA,AJ,6,O
82 Yasuo Sato, 'Direct Costing: A New Form and an Example', *The Hosei Journal of Business*, 1988, 1. AA,AJ,1,O
83 Yasuo Sato, 'Management Accounting Systems in the New Manufacturing Environment: Based on Robert A. Howell's papers', *The Hosei Journal of Business*, 1988, 4. AA,AJ,3,O
84 Isao Iizuka, 'Non-linearity of Costs in Pricing Decisions', *Fukuyama Economic Review*, 1988, 12. AA,AJ,6,O

85 X.P. Wang, 'Development of PERT Cost in Management Accounting', *The Keizai Ronkyu*, Kyushu University, 1988, 11. AA,AJ,6,T

86 Shozo Tokinaga, 'A Consideration of Expert Systems for Economic Accounting Using Knowledge Bases', *Keizaigaku-Kenkyu*, Kyushu Daigaku, 1988, 2. AA,AJ,9,O

87 Michiharu Sakurai, 'Management Accounting Practices at FA Factories', *Business Review of the Senshu University*, 1988, 9. AA,AJ,3,T

88 Michiharu Sakurai, 'Cost Management in FA Factories', *The Annual Bulletin of Social Science, The Institute for Social Science: Senshu University*, 1988, 3. AA,AJ,1,O

89 Hiromasa Itani, 'Zur Kostenstellen – Deckungsbeitragsrechnung' *['Cost incurrence within a company']*, *The Annual Bulletin of Commercial Sciences*, Senshu University, 1988, 3. AA,AJ,1,O

90 Shozo Takeshita, 'Various Interpretations of the "Liability Reserves" in the Japanese Commercial Code', *Okayama Economic Review*, 1988, 1. AA,AJ,9,O

91 Yoshikazu Toyoshima, 'Some Comments on the Financial Statements of Mitsubishi Dockyard and Engine Works in 1899–1900', *Annual Report of the Economic Society: Tohoku University*, 1988, 1. AA,AJ,4,O

92 Makoto Kitaoka, 'An Integration of Direct Costing and Responsibility Accounting: A Consideration on the Evolution of the Contribution Approach in the 1950s and 1960s', *Annual Report of the Economic Society: Tohoku University*, 1988, 6. AA,AJ,1,O

93 Yoshikazu Toyoshima, 'Some Comments on Separate Details of Establishment Charges Account of Mitsubishi Dockyard and Engine Works in 1900', *Annual Report of the Economic Society: Tohoku University*, 1988, 6. AA,AJ,4,O

94 Yoshikazu Toyoshima, 'Some Comments on the Head Office Current Account Book of Nagasaki Dockyard and Engine Works in 1900', *Annual Report of the Economic Society: Tohoku University*, 1988, 9. AA,AJ,4,O

95 Yoshiro Ito, 'A Programmed Cost Assignment Sheet in a Process Cost System – LIFO', *The Researches in Management and Accounting*, Takushoku University, 1988, 3. AA,AJ,1,O

96 Seiki Sato, 'Disclosure of Segmental Profits – A Study on the SFAS no.14', *The Journal of Economic Studies*, The University of Tokyo, 1988, 11. AA,AJ,5,O

97 Toshiro Hiromoto, 'Purposes and Topics of Management Accounting Research', *The Hitotsubashi Review*, Hitotsubashi

University, 1988, 11. AA,AJ,3,O

98 Hiroshi Obata, 'Mellerowitz's Concept of "Kapitalikosten"', *The Hitotsubashi Review*, Hitotsubashi University, 1988, 11. AA,AJ,1,O

99 Kazumasa Yoshida, 'The Trend of CASB and Impacts on Cost Accounting Standards', *Keizai-Kenkyu-Ronshu*, Hiroshima Economic University, 1988, 3. AA,AJ,8,T

100 Setsuro Terado, 'An Allocation of Uncontrollable Costs for Performance Evaluation', *Hokei Ronshu*, Yamanashi University, 1988, 3. AA,AJ,5,T

101 Yoshiro Ito, 'A Programmed Cost Assignment Sheet in a Process Cost System', *The Review of Takushoku University*, 1988, 12. AA,AJ,1,O

102 Akira Yoshida, 'A Management Accounting Approach to Business Policies in Some International Enterprises', *Yokohama Business Review*, Yokohama National University, 1988, 3. AA,AJ,6,O

103 Tsugio Kohno, 'Opportunitatskosten und Managerial Accounting (1) – Geschichte und Idee sowie Pramissen und Anwendungsberliche des Opportunitatskostenprinzips' *['Opportunity costing: history, ideas, premises and areas of use']*, *Oita University Economic Review*, 1988, 1. AA,AJ,1,O

104 Tsugio Kohno, 'Opportunitatskosten und Managerial Accounting (2) – Standard – Grenzpreizpreisrechnung und Preispolitik' *['Opportunity costing, marginal costing and pricing policy']*, *Oita University Economic Review*, 1988, 2. AA,AJ,6,O

105 Shinichi Kourogi, 'Some Problems of F.W. Taylor and Cost Accounting Development', *Journal of Kyushu Kyoritsu University*, 1988, 7. AA,AJ,4,T

106 Kazuo Furuya, 'The Origin of the Controllership (1)', The *Journal of the Society for Studies on Industrial Economies*, Kurume University, 1988, 6. AA,AJ,9,O

107 Shikazo Hirashima, 'The Development of Accounting and Information Processing Systems', *Fukuoka University Review of Commercial Sciences*, 1988, 3. AA,AJ,9,O

108 Noriyuki Inoue, 'On the Stage of Completion of Work in Process for Process Costing', *The Bulletin of Control Research Institute*, Fukuoka University, 1988, 3. AA,AJ,1,O

109 Naoki Murata, 'Cost Accounting Used by the Ball-Bearing Company', *Journal of Liberal Arts and Economics*, Nagasaki Kenritsu Kokusai Keizai Daigaku Ronshu, 1988, 11. AA,AJ,1,O

110 Ichiro Mizuno, 'Management Accounting and Public Relations', *Keizaigaku-Ronshu of Kagoshima University*, 1988, 3. AA,AJ,3,O

111 Ichiro Mizuno, 'Modern Corporation and Value Added Management Accounting', *Keizaigaku-Ronshu of Kagoshima University*, 1988, 12. AA,AJ,3,O

112 Toshinori Sato, 'Considerations on Accounting Control', *Journal of Management and Accounting*, Aichi University, 1988, 2. AA,AJ,2,O

113 Yasuyuki Kazusa, 'The Journal of Commerce and Economics Railroad Accounting of the American Railroad in the 1950s', *The Meijo Shogaku*, Meijo University, 1988, 10. AA,AJ,4,O

114 Yasuyuki Kazusa, 'The Expansion Strategy of Louisville and Nashville Railroad Co. and Its Accounting Practice: Railroad Cost Accounting', *The Meijo Shogaku*, Meijo University, 1988, 11. AA,AJ,4,O

115 Toshiharu Nakane, 'The Movement on the Elimination of Waste in Industry and its Impact on Cost Accounting', *The Meijo Shogaku*, Meijo University, 1988, 11. AA,AJ,1,O

116 Toshinori Sato, 'New Manufacturing Environment and Cost Accounting', *The Journal of the Association of Legal, Political and Economic Sciences*, Hokei Ronshu, Aichi University, 1988, 11. AA,AJ,1,O

117 Ichiei Kohno, 'A Study of "Lower of Cost or Market"', *Economic Journal*, Daito Bunka University, 1988, 9. AA,AJ,1,O

118 Kazumichi Suzuki and Takaaki Suzuki, 'The Proper Distribution of Expense Burden by A.H. Church', *Economic Journal*, Daito Bunka University, 1988, 9. AA,AJ,4,O

119 Masayoshi Kamei, 'Multinational Corporations and International Accounting – The Impact of MNC on the Development of International Accounting', *The Journal of Economic and Business Studies of Ryukyu University*, 1988, 3. AA,AJ,9,O

120 Masaki Hishiguchi, 'DSS and Management Accounting Information – Focusing on M.S.S. Marton's Opinions (2)', *Kenkyu-Kiyo*, Ryukoku University, 1988, 3. AA,AJ,3,T

121 Tadashi Shimura, 'On the Redesign of Cost Accounting Systems', *The Review of Business Administration*, Soka Keiei Ronshu, 1988, 3. AA,AJ,1,O

122 Tokio Ohnishi, 'The Subjects of Direct Costing – A Study of the Problems for Practice', *Meiji Accounting Review*, 1988, 3. AA,AJ,1,O

123 Hiroyuki Yamaura, 'Entwicklung der Kostenrechnung in GDR' *['The development of cost calculation in East Germany']*, *Meiji Accounting Review*, 1988, 3. AA,AJ,4,O

124 Kazuo Ohsawa, 'Eine Wiederbetrachtung uber das Verursachungsprinzipin der Kalkulation' *['Reviewing the principle*

of cause and responsibility'], *Meiji Accounting Review*, 1988, 3. AA,AJ,2,O

125 Atsuhiko Suzuki, Yoshinori Kato, Masaaki Takamatsu and Koji Matsuura, 'Business Games by PC', *The Annual Bulletin of the Institute of Industrial Management*, Rissho University, 1988, 6. AA,AJ,9,O

126 Keiichi Hasegawa, 'Reconsideration of Subsidiaries and Decisions – in a Context of Responsibility Accounting', *The Journal of Business and Economics*, Shokei Ronshu, Waseda University, 1988, 12. AA,AJ,2,O

127 Osamu Nishizawa, 'A Survey Report on Corporate and Interest Cost in Some Leading Japanese Corporations' (Research Papers), *Waseda Business Review*, Waseda University, 1988, 12. AA,AJ,1,O

128 Yukiro Iino, 'Environmental Change and Performance Evaluation – Towards New Cost Accounting Systems', *Keizai Kenkyu Nenshi*, Tohoku University, 1988. AA,AJ,5,O

1989

1 Tadashi Shimura, 'Direct Costing - Two Ancestors', *Information and Communications Studies*, Bunktyo University, 1989. AA,AJ,1,O

2 Kingo Imai, 'Financial Planning for Diversification', *Accounting Research*, Chuo University, 1989, 11. AA,AJ,6,O

3 Hitoshi Yanagita, 'Das geschichtliehe untersuchung des managerial accounting in Deutschland' *['A historic survey of management accounting in Germany']*, *Accounting Research*, Chuo University, 1989, 11. AA,AJ,4,O

4 Noriaki Kishikawa, 'A Statement of Basic Accounting Theory and Management Accounting', *The Annual Bulletin of the Institute of Business Research*, Chuo University, 1989. AA,AJ,3,O

5 Yasumasa Kondo, 'On the Contingency Theory of Budgetary Control Systems', *Doshisha Shogaku*, 1989, 2. AA,AJ,2,O

6 Yasumasa Kondo, 'The Shift in Cost Management – From Technology-driven Management Systems to Market-driven Management Systems', *Doshisha Shogaku*, 1989, 3. AA,AJ,1,O

7 Yasumasa Kondo, 'Some Observations on Management Accounting in a Japanese Manufacturing Company', *Doshisha Shogaku*, 1989, 9. AA,AJ,7,O

8 Akihiro Koyama, 'A Note on Uncertainty and Budgetary Control', *The Journal of the Department of Economics*, Gakushuin University, 1989, 3. AA,AJ,2,O

9 Hiroshi Fukuda, 'Comparison of the Capital Investments of Japanese Firms and Those of American Firms – Based on a

Questionnaire', *The Hosei Journal of Business*, 1989, 1. AA,AJ,6,O

10 Yasuo Sato, 'Germination, Formation and Development of Managerial Accounting in the USA', *The Hosei Journal of Business*, 1989, 7. AA,AJ,4,O

11 Kiyoshi Okamoto, 'Re-examination of Cost Accounting Standards in Japan', *Accounting*, 1989, 1. AA,AJ,8,O

12 Yutaka Kato, 'Case Research in Cost Accounting Studies', *Accounting*, 1989, 1. AA,AJ,1,O

13 Takao Makito, 'A Re-examination of Japanese Cost Accounting Standards', *Accounting*, 1989, 1. AA,AJ,8,O

14 Michiharu Sakurai, 'Cost Accounting for Software and its Relation to Cost Accounting Standards in Japan', *Accounting*, 1989, 1. AA,AJ,8,O

15 Kengo Kobayashi, 'A Reappraisal of the Cost Accounting Standards – Diversification or Unification in Cost Accounting?', *Accounting*, 1989, 1. AA,AJ,8,O

16 Tetsuo Kobayashi, 'Perceived Effectiveness of Budgetary Control Systems in Japanese Industry', *Accounting*, 1989, 1. AA,AJ,2,O

17 Toshiro Hiromoto, 'On the Development of Management Accounting Research in the USA', *Accounting*, 1989, 1. AA,AJ,9,O

18 Hiroshi Ito and Yoshihiro Ito, 'Cost Analysis for Competitive Advantage – A New Horizon of Cost Accounting Research', *Accounting*, 1989, 5. AA,AJ,1,O

19 Yoshitaka Kobayashi, 'Decision-making in Organisations and Management Accounting', *Accounting*, 1989, 5. AA,AJ,6,O

20 Hiroshi Obata, 'Entotehung der Kostenthorie in Deutschland' *['The origin of cost theory in Germany']*, *Accounting*, 1989, 5. AA,AJ,4,O

21 Hiroshi Ito and Yoshihiro Ito, 'Cost Analysis for Competitive Advantage – A New Horizon of Cost Accounting Research', *Accounting*, 1989, 6. AA,AJ,1,O

22 Yoshiho Tanaka and Shinichi Inoue, 'High-variety Production and Tender of Cost Accounting Practices for a Few Decades in Japan', *Accounting*, 1989, 7. AA,AJ,1,O

23 Yasuo Sato, 'Re-examination of the Essence and Function of Managerial Accounting', *Accounting*, 1989, 11. AA,AJ,3,O

24 Toshiro Hiromoto, 'A Re-examination of the Management Accounting System', *Accounting*, 1989, 11. AA,AJ,3,O

25 Masao Tsuji, 'Towards Redesigning New Management Accounting Systems with Information Technology', *Accounting*, 1989, 11. AA,AJ,3,O

26 Yoshiharu Fukushima, 'Notes on the History of Prime Cost in Great Britain', *Accounting*, 1989, 11. AA,AJ,4,O

27 Shuji Mizoguchi, 'The Function of a Management Accounting System in Organised Anarchy', *Accounting*, 1989, 12. AA,AJ,3,O

28 Kengo Kobayashi, 'Cost Accounting Standards', *Kigyokaikei*, 1989, 1. AA,CJ,8,O

29 Masaaki Miyamoto, 'The Latest Trends and Issues in Cost Management', *Kigyokaikei*, 1989, 2. AA,CJ,1,T

30 Masayasu Tanaka, 'Cost Management of New Product Development in Japanese Companies', *Kigyokaikei*, 1989, 2. AA,CJ,1T

31 Shinichi Inoue, 'JIT Production Systems and Cost Management', *Kigyokaikei*, 1989, 2. AA,CJ,1,T

32 Yasuhiro Kadota, 'Factory Automation and Cost Reduction – Case Study of the Daihatsu Automobile Industry', *Kigyokaikei*, 1989, 2. AA,CJ,1,T

33 Michiharu Sakurai, 'Cost Management for Software in Japanese Companies', *Kigyokaikei*, 1989, 2. AA,CJ,1,T

34 Kazaki Hamada, 'Profit Management System by the Amoeba Method – Case Study of Kyocera Co.', *Kigyokaikei*, 1989, 2. AA,CJ,5,T

35 Kyosuke Sakate, 'Profit Planning and DSS – Profit System Planning by MATPLAN', *Kigyokaikei*, 1989, 2. AA,CJ,6,T

36 Takeyuki Tani, 'The Realities of Transfer Pricing and Allocation of Headquarter Expenses in Japanese Companies', *Kigyokaikei*, 1989, 2. AA,CJ,6,T

37 Takayuki Asada, 'Comparative Study on Budgeting in Japan and the USA', *Kigyokaikei*, 1989, 7. AA,CJ,2,T

38 Yoshiho Tanaka, 'A Survey of the Current Situation and Trends in Japanese Cost Management', *Kigyokaikei*, 1989, 9. AA,CJ,1,T

39 Kengo Kobayashi, 'Unsolved Issues and Areas of Management Accounting', *Kigyokaikei*, 1989, 10. AA,CJ,3,T

40 Yoshitaka Kobayashi, 'Change of Environment and Management Accounting', *Kigyokaikei*, 1989, 10. AA,CJ,3,T

41 Yasuhiro Kadota, 'Profit and Cost Management by Recent Divisional Organisational Systems', *Kigyokaikei*, 1989, 11. AA,CJ,6,T

42 Yoshitaka Kijima, 'The Concept of Cost Accounting for Quality', *Kigyokaikei*, 1989, 11. AA,CJ,1,T

43 Michiharu Sakurai, 'Introduction to Factory Automation and Change in Management Accounting', *Sangyokeiri*, 1989, 1. AA,PJ,3,T

44 Yasuo Sato, 'Management Accounting for Overseas Companies', *Sangyokeiri*, 1989, 4. AA,PJ,3,T

45 Yasuo Morikawa, 'Interview with Professor Kurosawa –

Relationship between Cost Accounting Standard and Sangyo Keiri Institute', *Sangyokeiri*, 1989, 4. AA,PJ,8,T

46 Masaaki Imabayashi, 'Database of Segment Analysis in EDP Accounting System', *Sangyokeiri*, 1989, 7. AA,PJ,5,T

47 Michiharu Sakurai, 'The Investigation Commission's Reports of Cost Management Software', *Sangyokeiri*, 1989, 7. AA,PJ,1,T

48 Hiromitsu Sato, 'Relative Performance Evaluation – Beyond the Controllability Principle', *Sangyokeiri*, 1989, 10. AA,PJ,5,T

49 Makoto Yori, 'Current Budgeting Practices in Japan and the USA – Focusing on the Empirical Study by Srinivasan', *Sangyokeiri*, 1989, 10. AA,PJ,2,T

50 Kunitoshi Matsuba, 'Cost Accounting and Sales Tax', *Zeimutsushin*, 1989, 4. AA,CJ,1,T

51 Ryuji Takeda, 'Historical Evidence of Cost Accounting by Current Cost', *Kokumin Keizai Zasshi*, Kobe University, 1989, 2. AA,AJ,4,O

52 Takeyuki Tani, 'Strategy, Organisational Structure and Management Accounting Systems', *Kokumin Keizai Zasshi*, Kobe University, 1989, 5. AA,AJ,3,O

53 Katsuto Inoue, 'Decomposition Method for Linear Programmes and the Analysis of Budgetary Management', *The Kagawa University Economic Review*, 1989, 12. AA,AJ,2,O

54 Shinichi Inoue, 'A Change of Manufacturing System and its Effectiveness to Cost Management – Comparison between Seiban, JIT and MRP', *Kenkyu Nenpo*, Kagawa University, 1989, 3. AA,AJ,1,T

55 Koichi Saito, 'The Development of the Application of Organisational Theory to Budget Management', *The Gakusen Management Review*, Aichi Gakusen University, 1989, 6. AA,AJ,2,O

56 Koichi Saito, 'Otley's Contingency Theory – Applications to Budget Systems', *The Gakusen Management Review*, Aichi Gakusen University, 1989, 7. AA,AJ,2,O

57 Mitsumasa Naka, 'Logistic Information System Cost Accounting', *Asahi Business Review*, Asahi University, 1989, 12. AA,AJ,1,O

58 Hitoshi Yanagita, 'Die Entwicklung des Managerial Accounting in Deutschland' *['The development of managerial accounting in Germany'], Annual Report, The Institute of Industrial Sciences*, Nagoya Gakuin University, 1989, 12. AA,AJ,3,O

59 Yoshihiko Nakamura, 'A Study of Direct Materials Costing in a Conversion Cost System', *Zyoyogakuen University Kenkyu Ronshu*, 1989, 3. AA,AJ,1,O

60 'Professor Akira Imura's Career and Works', *Shakai Kagaku*

Ronshu, Nagoya Keizai University, 1989, 3. AA,AJ,9,O

61 Toshio Kimura, 'Cash Flow Accounting and Performance Evaluation', *Shakai Kagaku Ronshu*, Nagoya Keizai University, 1989, 3. AA,AJ,5,O

62 Masaaki Miyamoto, 'On the Strategic Cost Analysis', *The Hikone Ronso*, Siga University, 1989, 1. AA,AJ,1,O

63 Kengo Kobayashi, 'The Integration of Profit Variance and Standard Cost Variance', *The Hikone Ronso*, Siga University, 1989, 1. AA,AJ,2,O

64 Masaaki Ryoto, 'Die Entwicklung der Grenzplankostenrechnung', *The Hikone Ronso*, Siga University, 1989, 1.AA,AJ,2,O

65 Junko Odagiri, 'Grenzplankostenrechnung in Krankenhausbertrieben' *['Standard direct costing in hospitals']*, *The Hikone Ronso*, Siga University, 1989, 12. AA,AJ,2,O

66 Masaaki Aoki, 'A Study of Joint Cost Allocations', *Papers of the Research of Commerce and Economics*, Hiroshima Shudo University, 1989, 3. AA,AJ,1,O

67 Hiroshi Obata, 'Integration of Cost Theory into Cost Accounting', *Keiei Kodo*, Itotsubashi University, 1989, 12. AA,AJ,1,O

68 Yoshihiko Nakazaki, 'Strategic Allocation of Business Analysis', *Keiei Kodo*, Itotsubashi University, 1989, 12. AA,AJ,9,O

69 Setsumaro Yokoyama, 'Study of Cost Accounting in Daily Farm Management', *Rakuno Gakuen University*, Kiyo, 1989, 10. AA,AJ,1,O

70 Makoto Yori, 'An Application of Agency Theory to Management Accounting', *The Journal of Ryutsu Keizai University*, 1989, 9. AA,AJ,3,O

71 Makoto Yori, 'The Empirical Study of Budgeting in the USA by Srinivasan', *The Journal of Ryutsu Keizai University*, 1989, 12. AA,AJ,2,O

72 Kazuo Oosawa, 'Uber Schmalenbach Verrenchnungspreise' *['Schmalenbach and transfer prices']*, *Meiji University Daigakuin Kiyo*, Shogakuhen, 1989, 2. AA,AJ,5,O

73 Noriyuki Chikada, 'On the Role of the Concept of Profit for the Evaluation of Business Activities', *Memoir of the Graduate School*, Meiji University, 1989, 2. AA,AJ,5,O

74 Satoshi Yoshimura, 'On the Evolution of Direct Costing', *Memoir of the Graduate School*, Meiji University, 1989, 2. AA,AJ,4,O

75 Nobumasa Yamamoto, 'A Study on the Financial Performance Evaluation of Foreign Subsidiaries', *The Bulletin of the Institute for Research of Accounting*, 1989, 1. AA,AJ,5,O

76 Yoshio Maeda, 'Japanese Cost Accounting in the Cradle Years', *Keiei Keiri*, Kokushikan University, 1989, 4. AA,AJ,4,O

77 Sadao Kondo, 'The New Expansion of JNR's Economic Calculation System – A Critique of "Research Paper"', *Komazawa Business Review*, 1989, 3. AA,AJ,9,O

78 Hiroshi Sakaguchi, 'Innovation in Manufacturing Process and Changes of Cost Accounting System – An Investigation of Japanese and US Firms', *Journal of Economics*, Josai University, 1989, 9. AA,AJ,1,O

79 Takao Naito, 'On the Treatment of Personal Changes in French Accounting', *Seijo University Economic Papers*, 1989, 9. AA,AJ,9,O

80 Kengo Kobayashi, 'A Bibliography of Business Budgeting (3)', *Aoyama Journal of Business*, 1989, 3. AA,AJ,2,O

81 Kengo Kobayashi, 'Types of Marginal Income Variance – An Analytical Review', *Aoyama Journal of Business*, 1989, 6. AA,AJ,2,O

82 Kengo Kobayashi, 'A Theoretical Review of Marginal Income Analysis in Budgeting', *Aoyama Journal of Business*, 1989, 9. AA,AJ,2,O

83 Kengo Kobayashi, 'A Bibliography of Business Budgeting (4), (5)', *Aoyama Journal of Business*, 1989, 9; 1989, 11. AA,AJ,2,O

84 Takao Tanaka, 'Early Management Control in a Japanese Industrial Company – Mitsubishi Company, 1894–1897', *The Journal of Tokyo Keizai University*, 1989, 9. AA,AJ,4,O

85 Hirosi Obata, 'Future Directions for Cost Theory and Cost Accounting', *Hitotsubashi Ronso*, 1989, 4. AA,AJ,1,O

86 Toshiro Hiromoto, 'Some Cases – Linkages Between Accounting and Strategy', *Hitotsubashi Ronso*, 1989, 5.AA,AJ,3,O

87 Jusaku Ushio, 'Management of Overhead Cost', *Shokei Ronshu*, Chiba Keizai Junior College, 1989, 3. AA,AJ,1,O

88 Kazumasa Yoshida, 'The Rebirth of CASB', *Hiroshima Keizaidaigsku Keizai Kenkyu Ronshu*, 1989, 6. AA,AJ,8,O

89 Sadao Matsuyoshi, 'The Arguments on the Use of the LIFO Method', *Yamaguchi Journal of Economics, Business Administration and Law*, 1989, 7. AA,AJ,1,O

90 Hiroshi Ito, 'Innovation and Management Accounting', *Shogaku Ronshu*, Fukushima University, 1989, 3. AA,AJ,3,O

91 Koji Miyoshi, 'The Nature of Standard Costing Systems (2)', *Shogaku Ronshu*, Fukushima University, 1989, 7. AA,AJ,2,O

92 Koji Miyoshi, 'The Character of Standard Cost Accounting – Research Study Based on Heysman's Calculation Example', *Shogaku Ronshu*, Fukushima University, 1989, 11. AA,AJ,2,T

93 Naoki Murata, 'Cost Estimate and Decision-making', *Tyosa to Kenkyu*, Nagasaki Kenritsu International University, 1989, 3. AA,AJ,6,O

94 Masaaki Yamashita, 'The Cost Accounting of Mitsubishi Dockyard and Engine Works in the Early Years of Showa Era', *Journal of Business and Economics*, Nagasaki University, 1989, 3. AA,AJ,4,O

95 Ichiro Mizuno, 'A Study of Added Value Break-even Chart', *Keizaigaku-Ronshu of Kagoshima University*, 1989, 3. AA,AJ,6,O

96 Nobutoshi Nagaya, 'A Study of the Significance of Project Cost in Cost Accounting Systems', *The Business Review of Miyazaki Sangyo*, Keiei University, 1989, 3. AA,AJ,1,O

97 Seiken Takaoka, 'Characteristics of Management Accounting Information', *Oiu Journal of International Studies*, 1989, 3. AA,AJ,3,O

98 Masanobu Kosuga, 'An Introduction to Behavioural Research on Budgeting', *Journal of Administration*, Kwansai Gakuin University, 1989, 1. AA,AJ,2,O

99 Masanobu Kosuga, 'An Examination of Managerial Behaviour and Budget Slack within an Expectancy Theory Framework', *Journal of Business Administration*, Kwansai Gakuin University, 1989, 10. AA,AJ,2,O

100 Sadao Mitsuoka, 'Cost Accounting at the Turn of the Century in Britain and the USA (3), (4)', *Konan Business Review*, 1989, 1. 1989, 3. AA,AJ,4,O

101 Hiroshi Sakashita, 'Fundamentals of Joint Cost Accounting', *Shodai Ronshu*, Kobe University, 1989, 2. AA,AJ,1,O

102 Sadao Takatera, 'Organisational Legitimacy of Joint Management Accounting', *The Economic Review*, Kyoto University, 1989, 1. AA,AJ,3,O

103 Isao Iizuka, 'Cost Accounting in Factory Automation', *The Fukuyama Economic Review*, 1989, 3. AA,AJ,1,O

104 Isao Iizuka, 'Cost Accounting Adaptive to Environmental Changes', *The Fukuyama Economic Review*, 1989, 9. AA,AJ,1,O

105 Isao Iizuka, 'On the New Business Environment', *The Fukuyama Economic Review*, 1989, 9. AA,AJ,9,O

106 Hiroshi Tsuda, 'An Analytical Approach to the Objectives in a Business Budget System', *Meiji Gakuin Ronso*, Keikenkyu, 1989, 1. AA,AJ,2,O

107 Yasunari Iwata, 'One Trial of Improving Financial Position', *Meiji Gakuin Ronso*, Keiei Kenkyu, 1989, 1. AA,AJ,9,T

108 Kazunari Ito and Michiharu Sakurai, 'Types of Industry and Management Accounting Practices in Japan', *Senshu Keieigaku Ronshu*, 1989, 10. AA,AJ,7,O

109 Hiromasa Itani, 'Zur Deckungsbeitragsrechnung – Ein Teminologischer Vorschlag' *['Contribution-based costing – A logical suggestion']*, *Senshu Shogaku Ronshu*, 1989. AA,AJ,1,O

110 Hiroshi Okano, 'History of Cost Accounting by Murray C Wells – A Review Essay (3)', *Business Review*, Osaka City University, 1989, 4. AA,AJ,4,O

111 Hendricks, James A., 'Applying Cost Accounting to Factory Automation', *St. Paul's Economic Journal*, 1989, 6. AA,AJ,1,O

112 Reiji Shikida, 'Cost Accounting on the Postal Utility', *St Paul's Economic Journal*, 1989, 6. AA,AJ,1,O

113 Hiroshi Adachi and Reiji Shikida (eds), 'A New Approach to Cost Accounting', *St Paul's Economic Journal*, 1989, 3. AA,AJ,1,O

114 Masahiro Nakayama, 'Changes in the Operating Leverage Concept', *Senshu Keiei Kenkyu Nenpo*, 1989, 2. AA,AJ,9,T

115 Michiharu Sakurai, 'New Trends of Cost Management in the USA – Activity-based Costing', *Senshu Keiei Kenkyu Nenpo*, 1989, 2. AA,AJ,1,T

116 Yoshihiro Ito, 'The Multi-dimensions of Organisation and Management', *Seikei University Keizaigakubu Ronshu*, 1989, 9. AA,AJ,9,O

117 Tsutae Ishiyama, 'Contemporary Subjects in Cost Accounting – A Plan of Activity Costing', *The Journal of the Department of Economics of Obirin University*, 1989, 6. AA,AJ,1,O

118 Franke Reimund, 'A Process Model for Costing', *Nenpo Zyoho Kenkyu*, Soka University, 1989, 3. AA,AJ,1,O

119 Yoshikazu Sunada, 'A Study of the Evaluation of Corporate Performance by Electric and Electronics Corporations in Japan by Canonical Correlation Analysis', *The Soka Economic Studies Quarterly*, 1989, 3. AA,AJ,5,O

120 Kazuo Arai, 'Impact of Information Asymmetry on Performance in Participative Budgeting', *Hirosaki University Keizal Kenkyu*, 1989, 12. AA,AJ,2,O

121 Nashisa Sueishi, 'What are Distorts in Contemporary Cost Accounting? – A Review of Cooper and Kaplan's Article', *The Review of the Osaka University of Commerce*, 1989, 6. AA,AJ,1,O

122 Michio Nakamura, 'Leistungsbewertung und Nettoproduktion – Kennziffer des Kombinats und Betriebs in der DDR' *['Appraisal of net output results and ratios in East Germany'], Meiji Accounting Review*, 1989, 6. AA,AJ,5,O

123 Hiroaki Tatebe, 'On Cost Accounting at the Japanese Naval Arsenal', *Meiji Accounting Review*, 1989, 6. AA,AJ,4,O

124 Keiichi Hasegawa, 'Strategic Aspects of Subsidiaries – A New Perspective in Group Management Accounting', *The Bulletin of the Graduate School of Commerce*, Waseda University, 1989, 3. AA,AJ,5,O

125 Hiroyuki Goto, 'Evaluation of Divisional Performance by Residual Income Method', *The Bulletin of the Graduate School of*

Commerce, Waseda University, 1989, 3. AA,AJ,5,O

126 Yoshihiro Saruyama, 'The Usefulness of Advertising Budgeting Systems', *The Bulletin of the Graduate School of Commerce*, Waseda University, 1989, 12. AA,AJ,2,O

127 Tetsu Ono, 'Impacts of Management Accounting by Factory Automation', *The Bulletin of the Graduate School of Commerce*, Waseda University, 1989, 6. AA,AJ,3,O

128 Akiyoshi Nakamura, 'Rational Cost Variance Investigation *Rules', The Journal of Business and Economics*, Graduate School of Commerce, Waseda University, 1989, 6. AA,AJ,2,O

129 Yoshihide Iwabuchi, 'A Review of Recent Cost Accounting Studies', *The Journal of Business and Economics*, Graduate School of Commerce, Waseda University, 1989, 10. AA,AJ,1,O

130 Tetsu Ono, 'The Meaning of Quality Costs in the Age of Factory Automation', *The Journal of Business and Economics*, Graduate School of Commerce, Waseda University, 1989, 10. AA,AJ,1,O

131 Osamu Nishizawa, 'Cost Accounting, Cost Management and Profit Management in Corporate Departments', *The Waseda Commercial Review*, 1989, 1. AA,AJ,1,O

132 Morihiko Umeda, 'A Study of Volume Measures of Budget Flexibility', *Mita Business Review*, Keio University, 1989, 8. AA,AJ,2,O

133 Misao Yamaguchi, 'The "Achievement" Concept and Cost Accounting', *Mita Business Review*, Keio University, 1989, 12. AA,AJ,1,O

134 Yoshitaka Kobayashi, 'The Logical Structure of Cost Management', *Mita Business Review*, Keio University, 1989, 12. AA,AJ,1,O

135 Setsuro Terado, 'Changes in Cost Objects and Cost Accounting', *The Yamanashi Economic and Law Review*, 1989, 3. AA,AJ,1,O

136 Mutsuko Tokoi, 'Schmalenbach und die Wirkung' *['The consequences of Schmalenbach'], Kenkyu Ronsyu,* Tokyo Metropolitan College of Commerce, 1989, 3. AA,AJ,9,O

137 Kenji Aizaki, 'Accounting and Institutionalism', *The Kokugakuin University Economic Review*, 1989, 2. AA,AJ,9,O

138 Shuji Mizoguchi, 'The Structure of a Management Accounting System in the Garbage Can Model', *Yokohama Business Review*, 1989, 3. AA,AJ,3,O

139 Takeo Yoshikawa, 'Comparative Study of Cost Accounting Systems in Japan and the UK (1), (2)', *Yokohama Business Review*, 1989, 9. 1989, 12. AA,AJ,1,O

140 Hiroshi Ito, Shi Ren Jin and Lin Bao Gui, 'Responsibility

Accounting with the Internal Banking System in China', *The Bulletin of Yokohama City University*, 1989, 3. AA,AJ,2,O

141 Toshinori Sato, 'Considerations on Quality Costs', *Journal of Management and Accounting*, Aichi University, 1989, 2. AA,AJ,1,O

142 Atsumi Murata, 'A Study of a Conceptual Framework for Management Accounting in Anthony – The Use of Mintzberg's Organisation Theory in Management Accounting', *Economic Science*, Nagoya University, 1989, 3. AA,AJ,3,O

143 Tsuneto Miyosawa, 'Financial Accounting and Managerial Accounting', *The Bimonthly Journal of Ritsumeikan University*, 1989, 3. AA,AJ,3,O

144 Yukihiro Iino, 'A Basic Study on Operating Controls in Cost Accounting – Non-financial Performance Measures in the New Manufacturing Environment', *Keizai Kenkyu Nenshi*, Tohoku Gakuin University, 1989. AA,AJ,5,O

1990

1 Hiromasa Itani, 'Ergebniscontroling und Deckungsbeitrags – Flubrechnung' *['Controlling performance and contribution costing'], Senshu Shogaku Ronshi*, 1990, 3. AA,AJ,2,O

2 Isao Iizuka, 'Multiple Cost Accounting Systems in the New Manufacturing Environment', *The Fukuyama Economic Review*, 1990, 3. AA,AJ,3,O

3 Kanji Miyamoto, 'Characteristics of Management Accounting for Overseas Companies', *Kigyokaikei*, 1990, 2. AA,CJ,3,T

4 Hidekazu Imaki, 'Globalisation of Business Firms and Performance Evaluation – Transfer Pricing', *Kigyokaikei*, 1990, 2. AA,CJ,5,T

5 Michiharu Sakurai, 'The Realities of Modern Overhead Cost Management', *Kigyokaikei*, 1990, 3. AA,CJ,1,T

6 Takao Tanaka, '"Kaizen" Budgeting in Toyota – Typical Japanese Budgeting', *Kigyokaikei*, 1990, 3. AA,CJ,2,T

7 Yoshitaka Kobayashi, 'Cost Management and Value Engineering', *Accounting*, 1990, 3. AA,AJ,1,O

8 Yasumasa Kondo, 'The Shift in Cost Management', *Accounting*, 1990, 4. AA,AJ,1,O

9 Takeyuki Tani, 'Corporate Strategy and Accounting for Control', *Accounting*, 1990, 5. AA,AJ,2,O

10 Noboru Ogura, 'The Role of Management Accounting under the Restructuring Strategy', *Accounting*, 1990, 6. AA,AJ,3,O

11 Katsunosuke Moroi, 'Cost Accounting Standard and its Legislating Process', *Sangyokeiri*, 1990, 1. AA,PJ,8,T

12 Kengo Kobayashi, 'The Limitation of Cost Management by Efficiency and an Extent of Operation-oriented Cost

Management', *Sangyokeiri*, 1990, 1. AA,PJ,1,T

13 Yoshitaka Kobayashi, 'A Relationship Between Cost Management and TQC', *Sangyokeiri*, 1990, 4. AA,PJ,1,T

14 Ryuji Takeda, 'Current Cost Accounting and Managerial Value Cost Accounting', *Zeimutsushin*, 1990, 5. AA,CJ,1,T

15 Kanji Miyamoto, 'A Study of Measuring Cash Flow from Foreign Operations: Its Relevance to Management in Multinational Corporations', *The Review of Economics and Business Management*, Kwansei Gakuin University, 1990, 3. AA,AJ,5,O

16 Yuji Oshita, 'Comparison of Performance Accounting of Japanese Firms and that of French Firms – Based on a Questionnaire', *The Hosei Journal of Business*, 1990, 1. AA,AJ,5,O

17 Kazuo Arai, 'Schools of Behavioural Accounting and Participative Budgeting Research', *Studies in the Humanities*, Hirosaki University, 1990, 3. AA,AJ,2,O

18 Yuta Hoshino, 'Accounting for Managing Automated Factories in Manufacturing Industries – Adapting Management Accounting to Factory Automation', *Studies in the Humanities*, Hirosaki University, 1990, 3. AA,AJ,3,O

19 Yoshijiro Nishida, 'On Rummel's Blockkostenrechnung (2)' *['On Rummel's block cost accounting']*, *The Doshisha Business Review*, 1990, 2. AA,AJ,1,O

20 Susumu Sato, 'Postulates of Cost Accounting Systems', *The Journal of Commerce*, Chuo University, 1990, 3. AA,AJ,1,O

21 Kozo Yamaguchi, 'Theorie des Datenbankorientiertes Rechnungswesens im BRD' *['The theory of databank-related accounting']*, *Nihon Keizai Junior College Kiyo*, 1990, 2. AA,AJ,3,O

22 Masahiro Nakayama, 'Changes of Overhead Cost Variance Analysis in the USA', *Sehshu Keiei Kenkyu Nenpo*, 1990, 2. AA,AJ,2,T

23 Yoshiharu Fukushima, 'Prime Cost System as a Stage in the History of Cost Accounting', *The Economic Review*, Otaru University, 1990, 3. AA,AJ,4,O

24 Noboru Harada, 'Conditional Investigation and Economic Performance Evaluation – An Agency Theory Perspective', *Review of Economics and Business*, Sapporo Gakuin University, 1990, 3. AA,AJ,5,O

25 Hiroshi Ikano, 'Management Accounting History – Some Japanese Contributions', *Business Review*, Osaka City University, 1990, 1. AA,AJ,4,O

26 Daisuke Watanabe, 'Diffusion of Management Accounting', *Journal of Osaka University of Economics*, 1990, 3. AA,AJ,3,0

27 Yoshihiko Nakamura, 'A Study of Management Accounting',

Zyoyo Gakuen Hamam Atsu University Kenkyu Ronshu, 1990, 3. AA,AJ,3,O

28 Toshinori Sato, 'Factory Automation and Changes in Cost Accounting', *Aichi Journal of Business*, 1990, 2. AA,AJ,1,O

29 Morihiko Umeda, 'Cost Control by Standard Cost and by Budget', *The Journal of Gifu College of Economics*, 1990, 3. AA,AJ,2,O

30 Yutaka Kato, 'Business Strategies and SIS – A Linkage by Management Accounting', *Operations Research*, 1990, 6. AA,AJ,9,T

31 Masao Ueno, 'The Evolution of Management in Canada – A Verification of Relevance Lost by John J. Williams and Alan A. Richardson', *The Bulletin of the Faculty of Economics*, Wako University, 1990, 2. AA,AJ,4,O

32 Masao Kawano, 'Satellite Accounts and Social Responsibility Accounting', *Yokohama Business Review*, 1990, 3. AA,AJ,3,O

33 Takeo Yoshikawa, 'Comparative Study of Cost Accounting Systems in Japan and the UK (3)', *Yokohama Business Review*, 1990, 3. AA,AJ,1,O

34 Kiyoshi Yamaya, 'Thatcher "Revolution" in Public Management – "Agency" and Performance Indicator', *Kokugaku in University Kiyo*, 1990, 3. AA,AJ,5,O

35 Yoshitaka Kobayashi, 'A Tentative Framework for the Study of Cost Management', *Hitotsubashi Ronso*, 1990, 5. AA,AJ,1,O

36 Yoshihide Iwabuchi, 'Performance Evaluation in Multinational Corporations – The Impact of Exchange Risk on Budgeting', *The Bulletin of the Graduate School of Commerce*, Waseda University, 1990. AA,AJ,2,O

37 Osamu Nishizawa, 'Field Study and Techniques in Manpower Cost Management', *The Waseda Commercial Review*, 1990, 2. AA,AJ,1,O

38 Kengo Kobayashi, 'A Bibliography of Budgeting (6)', *Aoyama Journal of Business*, 1990, 3. AA,AJ,2,O

39 Jiro Asaba, 'Some Problems in Formulating Accounting Theory', *The Journal of Musashi University*, 1990, 3. AA,AJ,9,O

40 Toshiyasu Kato, 'A Review of the Relevant Cost Concept', *The Economic Review of Komazawa University*, 1990, 3. AA,AJ,6,O

41 Naohisa Sueishi, 'The Necessity of a New Cost System – On a View of Robin Cooper's Article', *The Review of the Osaka University of Commerce*, 1990, 1. AA,AJ,1,O

42 Yoshikazu Toyoshima, 'Some Comments on the Organisation of Mitsubishi Dockyard and Engine Works Enforced in 1908', *Annual Report of the Economic Society, Tohoku University*, 1990, 3. AA,AJ,4,O

43 Kozo Yamaguchi, 'Die Bedeutung der Zweckneutralen Grendrechnung' *['The meaning of purpose-neutral calculation']*, *Nihon Keizai Junior College Kiyo*, 1990, 7. AA,AJ,9,O
44 Hisashi Mori, 'The Relationship Between Annual Changes in Cost of Goods Sold Ratio and those of Other Cost Ratios: An Application of Canonical Correlation Analysis', *Meiji University Shakaikagaku Kenkyu Kiyo*, 1990, 3. AA,AJ,5,O
45 Yasumasa Kondo, 'The Evolution of the Main Issues in the Quality Cost Concept', *The Doshisha Business Review*, 1990, 7. AA,AJ,1,O
46 Seiken Kataoka, 'The Role of Full Cost Accounting Information', *Oiu Journal of International Studies*, 1990, 9. AA,AJ,1,O
47 Takao Tanaka, 'New Product Development and Target Cost in Automobile Companies', *Kigyokaikei*, 1990, 10. AA,CJ,1,T
48 Yasuo Sato, 'Cost Accounting and Profit Management in Hi-Tech Companies', *Kigyokaikei*, 1990, 10. AA,CJ,1,T
49 Yoshitaka Kobayashi, 'A Countermeasure for Environmental Changes at Electric Manufacturing Companies – Management Accounting in Toshiba', *Kigyokaikei*, 1990, 10. AA,CJ,7,T
50 Shuji Mizoguchi, 'Strategic Planning Support and Management Accounting – Functions of DSS Model in an Energy Company', *Kigyokaikei*, 1990, 10. AA,CJ,6,T
51 Hiroshi Ishizuka, 'A Choice of Management Accounting Systems', *Kigyokaikei*, 1990, 12. AA,CJ,3,T
52 Yutaka Kato, '*Genka-keikaku* and Managerial Accounting', *Kokuminkeizai Zasshi*, Kobe University, 1990, 8. AA,AJ,3,O
53 Takeyuki Tani, 'Accounting for Performance and Strategic Management', *Kokumin Keizai Zasshi*, Kobe University, 1990, 11. AA,AJ,5,O
54 Kazumichi Suzuki, 'The Establishment of Costing in Britain: From the Standpoint of the Social System', *Accounting*, 1990, 11. AA,AJ,4,O
55 Kanji Miyamoto, 'Classifying the Management of Multinational Corporations and Management Accounting', *Accounting*, 1990, 11. AA,AJ,5,O
56 Michiharu Sakurai, 'Accounting Principles of ABC and its Character', *Sangyokeiri*, 1990, 7. AA,PJ,1,T
57 Yoshihiro Ito, 'Cost Management and Strategic Cost Analysis – Study on a Two-way Understanding of Cost Drivers', *Sangyokeiri*, 1990, 7. AA,PJ,1,T
58 Tomio Muraoka, 'Cost Accounting and Cost Management in Electric and Machine Manufacturing Companies', *JICPA Journal*, 1990, 8. PA,PJ,1,T

59 Shuichi Fujimura, 'Cost Accounting and Cost Management in the Air Cargo Industry', *JICPA Journal*, 1990, 9. PA,PJ,1,T
60 Kanji Miyamoto, 'A Countermeasure for Currency Fluctuation and Management Accounting', JICPA Journal, 1990, 10. AA,PJ,3,T
61 Sentaro Kashima, 'Cost Accounting and Cost Management in the Construction Industry', *JICPA Journal*, 1990, 10. AA,PJ,1,T
62 Michiharu Sakurai, 'Cost Accounting and Cost Management – Life Cycle Costing', *JICPA Journal*, 1990, 11. AA,PJ,1,T
63 Shiro Inamoto, 'A Study of the Scope and Method of Managerial Accounting in Farm Corporations', *Nogyo Keisangaku Kenkyu*, Kyoto University, 1989, 12. AA,AJ,7,O
64 Wang Xiao Ping, 'A Critical Approach to Current Management Accounting', *Keizai Kenkyu*, Kyushu University, 1990, 3. AA,AJ,3,O
65 Koichi Sato, 'Regression Analysis for Management Accounting', *The Gakusen Management Review*, 1990, 9. AA,AJ,3,O
66 Yukihiro Matsuda and Masao Nakane, 'The Effects of Supervisor Attributions of Subordinate Poor Performance on Feedback', *Asahi Business Review*, 1990, 7. AA,AJ,5,O
67 Koji Yamamoto, 'An Application of Fuzzy Sets Theory to Accounting Cost Control', *The Journal of Economic Studies*, University of Osaka Prefecture, 1990, 9. AA,AJ,2,0
68 Yoshitaka Hazama, 'Uber Selbskostenrechnung und Preispolitik von E. Schmalenbach (2)' *['Schmalenbach's cost estimation in pricing policy']*, *Quarterly Review*, Nara Prefectural College, 1990, 1. AA,AJ,1,O
69 Yoshitaka Hazama, 'Uber Selbkostenrechnung und preispolitik von E. Schmalenbach (3)' *['Schmalenbach's cost estimation and pricing policy']*, *Quarterly Review*, Nara Prefectural College, 1990, 3. AA,AJ,1,O
70 Tomoaki Sonoda, 'Empirical Analysis of Cost Accounting in Japanese Software Companies – The Analysis of the Cost Reports in the Annual Report', *Mita Business Review*, Keio University, 1990, 8. AA,AJ,1,O
71 Tamio Fushimi and Yumiko Ashiwa, 'Tax Effect on Profitability of Capital Investment in Foreign Subsidiaries: Analytical Modelling Approach', *Keio Business Forum*, 1990, 3. AA,AJ,5,O
72 Hironori Ono, 'A Study of the Conditions for the Existence of Groves' Scheme – Applying the Resource Allocation Model under Uncertainty', *Shimonoseki City College Review*, 1990, 5. AA,AJ,6,O
73 Kengo Kobayashi, 'A Study of Cost Variances in Budget Profit Variance Analysis', *Aoyama Journal of Business*, 1990, 6.

AA,AJ,2,O
74 Mikio Tokai, 'Cost Information for Business Decision-making', *Aoyama Journal of Business*, 1990, 6. AA,AJ,2,O
75 Kengo Kobayashi, 'A Theoretical Review of Cost Variances in Budget Profit Variance Analysis', *Aoyama Journal of Business*, 1990, 8. AA,AJ,2,O
76 Shinichi Sugisawa, 'New Approach to Cost Management', *Rissho Management Review*, 1990, 3. AA,AJ,1,O
77 Nobumasa Shimizu, 'The Meaning of Opportunity Cost in Management Accounting', *The Review of the Osaka University of Commerce*, 1990, 6. AA,AJ,1,T
78 Tsugio Kono, 'Eine Anwendung der Deckungsbeitragsrechnung zur Optimale Produktions und Absatzplanung bei Kuppelproduktion' *['An application of marginal accounting for the optimisation of production and sales planning with joint product cost'], Oita University Economic Review*, 1990, 7. AA,AJ,1,O
79 Masami Motohashi, 'A Review of Control Concepts in Management Accounting', *Meiji Accounting Review*, 1990, 6. AA,AJ,2,O
80 Hiroaki Takebe, 'On the Three Papers on Cost Accounting in the Meiji Era', *Meiji Accounting Review*, 1990, 6. AA,AJ,4,O
81 Yasumichi Iizuka, 'A Study of Direct Product Profit', *Meiji Accounting Review*, 1990, 6. AA,AJ,1,O
82 Takao Sawamura, 'A Study of Real Cost', *Meiji Accounting Review*, 1990, 6. AA,AJ,1,O
83 Tetsu Ono, 'Conditions in Quality Costing's Realistic Applications – Basing Two Approaches', *The Journal of Business and Economics*, Graduate School of Commerce, Waseda University, 1990, 3. AA,AJ,1,O
84 Akiyoshi Nakamura, 'Cost Allocation and the Information from Marginal Cost', *The Journal of Business and Economics*, Graduate School of Commerce, Waseda University, 1990, 3. AA,AJ,1,O
85 Takashi Shimizu, 'Transfer Pricing Standards Classified by Strategic Organisations', *The Waseda Commercial Review*, 1990, 7. AA,AJ,5,O
86 Keiichi Hasegawa, 'Reconsidering Robert S. Kaplan's Standpoint onManagment Accounting: Seeking a Research Agenda in the Area', *The Waseda Commercial Review*, 1990, 7. AA,AJ,3,O
87 Hideo Yazawa, 'The Development of Physical Distribution Mission Costing', *Senshu Shogaku Ronshu*, 1990, 9. AA,AJ,1,O
88 Satoshi Yoshimura, 'On the Origin of Direct Costing', *Memoir of the Graduate School*, Meiji University, 1990, 2. AA,AJ,4,O

89 Kono Ichiro, 'Development of Information Systems and Management Accounting', *The Chuo-Gakuin University Review of Economics and Commerce*, 1990. AA,AJ,3,O

90 Yukihiro Nakamura, 'A Study of Object Control Information', *The Journal of Economic Studies*, Toyama University, 1990, 11. AA,AJ,2,O

91 Takeo Yoshikawa, 'Comparative Study of Cost Accounting Systems in Japan and the UK (4), (5)', *Yokohama Business Review*, 1990, 6. 1990, 9. AA,AJ,1,O

92 Tadashi Shimura, 'Some Comments on the Applicability of Activity-Based Costing to Decision-making', *Information and Communications Studies*, Bunkyo University, 1990. AA,AJ,6,O

93 Yasumasa Kondo, 'Notes on Just-in-Time (2) – The Impact of JIT on Management Accounting Practices', *The Doshisha Business Review*, 1990, 12. AA,AJ,3,O

94 Eiichiro Kudo, 'A Factor in Relevance Lost of Management Accounting Systems', *Studies on the Social and Cultural Sciences*, Kagoshima University, 1990, 7. AA,AJ,3,O

95 Nobutoshi Nagaya, 'Cost Management in Kubota Inc.', *The Business Review of Miyazaki Sangyo Keiei University*, 1990, 9. AA,AJ,1,O

96 Masanobu Kozuka, 'An Analysis of Budgetary Biasing Behaviour', *Journal of Business Administration*, Kwansei Gakuin University, 1990, 12. AA,AJ,2,O

97 Masanobu Kozuka, 'Budgeting Practices in Japanese Industry – A Research Review', *Kwansei Gakuin University Annual Studies*, 1990, 12. AA,AJ,2,O

98 Genri Hisatomi, 'On the Significance of Laboratory Experimental Studies of Behavioural Managerial Accounting', *Kobe-Gakuin Economic Papers*, 1990, 9. AA,AJ,3,O

99 Isao Iizuka, 'Management-oriented Income Statements in the Third Industry', *The Fukuyama Economic Review*, 1990, 7. AA,AJ,5,O

100 Isao Iizuka, 'Decision Support Systems and Management Accounting (1)', *The Fukuyama Economic Review*, 1990, 11. AA,AJ,6,O

101 Yoshihiro Saruyama, 'The Effectiveness of Participative Budgeting – A Discussion on Brownell's Studies', *Ehime Economic Journal*, 1990, 11. AA,AJ,2,O

102 Yoshihiro Saruyama, 'The Impact of Environmental Uncertainty and Departmental Authority on the Perceived Importance of Advertising Measures', *The Economic Review Ehime University*, 1990, 11. AA,AJ,5,O

103 Kenji Miyanishi, 'Cash Flow Ratios and Principal Component

Analysis Regarding Performance Evaluation', *Osaka Economic Papers*, 1990, 9. AA,AJ,5,O

104 Makoto Yori, 'The International Perspective in Management *Accounting*', *The Hikone Ronso*, Siga University, 1990, 8. AA,AJ,3,O

105 Junko Odagiri, 'Cost Accounting in Service Industries', *The Hikine Ronso*, Siga University, 1990, 10. AA,AJ,1,O

106 Yuko Nishimura, 'The Determinants of Industrial Manpower Costs', *Kenkyu Ronso*, Tokyo Metropolitan Junior College of Commerce, 1990, 6. AA,AJ,1,O

107 Akitoshi Nakamura, 'The Aggregation of Signals and its Application to Accounting Problems', *The Bulletin of the Graduate School of Commerce*, Waseda University, 1990, 12. AA,AJ,9,O

108 Takashi Shimizu, 'Transfer Pricing to Serve a Purpose and to Adapt to the Environment', *The Bulletin of the Graduate School of Commerce*, Waseda University, 1990, 12. AA,AJ,5,O

109 Keiichi Hasegawa, '"Relevance Lost" and "Gap Between Theory and Practice" in Management Accounting', *The Bulletin of the Graduate School*, Waseda University, 1990, 12. AA,AJ,3,O

110 Ichiro Kono, 'Development of Technical Innovation and Management Accounting', *Bulletin of the Research Institute*, Chuo-Gakuin University, 1990, 10. AA,AJ,3,O

111 Masashi Hagino, 'The Realities of Performance Measurement Accounting of Order Production Enterprises in West Germany', *Bulletin of the Research Institute*, Chuo Gakuin University, 1990, 10. AA,AJ,5,O

112 Yasuo Sato, 'Germination, Formation and Development of Managerial Accounting in the USA (2)', *The Hosei Journal of Business*, 1990, 10. AA,AJ,4,O

113 Yoshiro Kimizuka, 'The Cost Accounting Regulations in Meiji 14 (1881) – On the "Bookkeeping Procedures" of the Printing Office of the Ministry of Finance', *Kaikeigaku Kenkyu*, Nihon University, 1990. AA,AJ,4,O

114 Fumiyasu Takahashi, 'An Empirical Study of Cost Accounting for Medium- and Small-sized Companies in Japan', *Kaikeigaku Kenkyu*, Nihon University, 1990. AA,AJ,7,O

115 Yasuyuki Fukuda, 'A Critical Essay on A.H. Church's Management Theory', *Journal of Business and Economics*, Kinki University, 1990, 11. AA,AJ,4,O

116 Hiroyoshi Higuchi, 'The Formation of Standard Cost Accounting and Corporate Strategy', *Journal of Law and Economics*, Iwate Prefectural Morioka College, 1990, 12. AA,AJ,2,O

117 Kengo Kobayashi, 'A Bibliography of Budgeting (7), (8)',

Aoyama Journal of Business, 1990, 11; 1991, 3. AA,AJ,2,O

118 Takanori Furuta, 'Inflation and Management Accounting – R.F. Vancil's Review', *Osaka Gakuin University Shogaku Ronshu*, 1990, 12. AA,AJ,3,O

119 Yoshitaka Hazama, 'Uber Selbstkostenrechnung und Preispolitik von E. Schmalenbach (4)' *['Schmalenbach's cost estimating and pricing policy'], Nara University of Commerce*, 1990, 12. AA,AJ,1,O

1991

1 Yasumasa Kondo, 'On Target Costing', *The Doshisha Business Review*, 1991, 2. AA,AJ,1,O

2 Kazuki Hamada, 'Management Planning Models Based on Structure Matrix', *The Commercial Review of Seinan Gakuin University*, 1991, 2. AA,AJ,6,O

3 Tsugio Kono, 'A Paradigm of Managerial Accounting Systems', *Oita University Economic Review*, 1991, 2. AA,AJ,3,O

4 Nobumasa Matsuo, 'Attitudes Towards Corporate Social Accountability in the United States', *The Business Review of Kansai University*, 1991, 2. AA,AJ,9,O

5 Kiyoshi Ogawa, 'Management Accounting Innovation in the New Manufacturing Environment – Based on Japanese Management Accounting Practice', *Accounting*, 1991, 2. AA,AJ,3,O

6 Noboru Ogura, 'Some Current Aspects of Quality Costing', *Accounting*, 1991, 2. AA,AJ,1,O

7 Takeo Yoshikawa, 'Cost Management of Japanese Industries – Current and Future', *Accounting*, 1991, 2. AA,AJ,1,O

8 Masayasu Tanaka, 'Cost Estimate Systems in the Computer Integrated Manufacturing (CIM) Age', *Accounting*, 1991, 2. AA,AJ,1,O

9 Akira Nishimura, 'A Comparative Study of Management Accounting in Japan and the United States', *Accounting*, 1991, 2. AA,AJ,7,O

10 Yasuo Sato, 'A Change in Cost Accounting – An American Case Study', *Accounting*, 1991, 2. AA,AJ,1,O

11 Ryoji Nishimura, 'A Study on Class Cost System', *Sangyokeiri*, 1991, 1. AA,PJ,1,T

12 Hiromasa Itani, 'Creation of a Dynamic Cost Concept', *Sehshu Shogaku Ronshu*, 1991, 3. AA,AJ,1,T

13 Lee, Gun Yung, 'A Contingency Model for Evaluating Cost Variance', *Bulletin of Faculty of Commerce*, Nagoya University of Commerce, 1991, 3. AA,AJ,2,O

14 Masakatsu Ooshima, 'A Comparative Study of Management Accounting Practice in the New Manufacturing Environment in Japan, Korea and the USA', *Asia University Management Review*, 1991, 3. AA,AJ,7,O

15 Masatoshi Uchida, 'On "A Positive Approach" to Budgetary Control by J.L. Peirce (1954)', *Hokkai-Gakuen University Journal of Economics*, 1991, 3. AA,AJ,2,O

16 Satoshi Yoshimura, 'On the Direct Costing Controversy', *The Journal of Ryutsu Keizai University*, 1991, 2. AA,AJ,1,O

17 Shigeru Kaneko, 'Business Planning and Project Management – A Study of Manufacturing Project Management', *The Social Science Review, Saitama University*, 1991, 2. AA,AJ,6,O

18 Osamu Nishizawa, 'The Allocation of Information System Costs to Users', *The Waseda Commercial Review*, 1991, 3. AA,AJ,1,O

19 Yasuo Sato, 'Cost Accounting in the Beer Industry – The Case of the Orion Beer Company', *The Hosei Journal of Business*, 1991, 1. AA,AJ,1,O

20 Maoki Murata, 'Accounting in the People's Republic of China', *Journal of Liberal Arts and Economics*, Nagasaki Prefectural University, 1991, 3. AA,AJ,7,O

21 Chikaki Sugihara, 'The Recognition and Control of Costs in Cost Accounting – On Transaction Costs and Discretionary Costs', *Oiu Journal of International Studies*, 1991, 3. AA,AJ,1,O

22 Isao Iizuka, 'Management Accounting Reports Design in Response to Technological Change', *Accounting*, 1991, 4. AA,AJ,3,O

23 Michiharu Sakurai, 'Change in the Business Environment and Management Accounting', *Accounting*, 1991, 5. AA,AJ,3,O

24 Isao Iizuka, 'Management Accounting Reports Design in Response to Technological Change', *Accounting*, 1991, 5. AA,AJ,3,O

25 Yuta Hoshino, 'The Manufacturer's CIM and the New Environment of Managerial Accounting: Empirical Research on Manufacturing Change in Japanese Industry', *Accounting*, 1991, 7. AA,AJ,3,O

26 Yoshihiro Ito, 'Measuring and Controlling Product Liability Costs', *Accounting*, 1991, 7. AA,AJ,1,O

27 Yukio Harada, 'A Study on Strategic Information and Management Accounting Information', *Accounting*, 1991, 8. AA,AJ,3,O

28 Hiromasa Itani, 'Zur Grundlegung Betriebswirtschaftliches Kostenbegriffs' *['The foundation of the definition of managerial cost']*, *Accounting*, 1991, 8. AA,AJ,1,O

29 Fujio Harada, 'Self-Appraising System for Corporate Social

Responsibilities', *Accounting*, 1991, 10. AA,AJ,9,O

30 Kenji Aizaki, 'Accounting and Environmental Problems', *Accounting*, 1991, 9. AA,AJ,9,O

31 Yoshitaka Kijima, 'Clark's Theory of Cost Accounting: Present-day Significance', *Accounting*, 1991, 9. AA,AJ,1,O

32 Takao Tanaka, 'Development of Management Accounting Systems in Japan – Case Study at Mitsubishi and Toyota', *Sangyokeiri*, 1991, 4. AA,PJ,7,O

33 Atsuo Takei, 'Creation and Application of Segment Accounting for Modern Management', *Sangyokeiri*, 1991, 7. AA,PJ,5,O

34 Kentaro Nomura, 'Value Added and Throughput Value Added – Based on French Business Accounting', *Sangyokeiri*, 1991, 7. AA,PJ,9,O

35 Yasuo Sato, 'A Survey of Management Accounting for Overseas Companies', *Sangyokeiri*, 1991, 7. AA,PJ,7,O

36 Yutaka Kato, Makota Yori, Hiroshi Okano, Yoshihide Iwabuchi, 'Development of New Management Accounting – Search for Global Management Accounting', *Sangyokeiri*, 1991, 7. AA,PJ,3,O

37 Genri Hisatomi, 'A Study of Responsibility Accounting', *Kobe-Gakuin Economic Papers*, 1991, 3. AA,AJ,2,O

38 Yoshihiro Saruyama, 'Participative Budgeting and Performance Evaluation (1)', *Ehime Economic Journal*, 1991, 7. AA,AJ,5,O

39 Michiyasu Nakajima, 'A History of Cost Accounting in Germany in the Middle of the Nineteenth Century – A Review of C.G. Gottschalk (1865)', *The Kagawa University Economic Review*, 1991, 3. AA,AJ,4,O

40 Masataro Arai, 'The Birth of Accounting Theory by Professor Kurosawa (2)', *Journal Faculty of Commerce Chkyo University*, 1991, 3. AA,AJ,4,O

41 Koji Yamamoto, 'An Application of Fuzzy Linear Programming in the Management Accounting Fields', *The Journal of Economic Studies*, University of Osaka Prefecture, 1991. AA,AJ,3,O

42 Masaaki Ryoto, 'Die Heutigen Aufgaben zu den Kostenrechnungssystemen' *['The contemporary function of costing systems']*, *The Hiroshima Economic Review*, 1991, 3. AA,AJ,1,O

43 Kenji Okano, 'On the Extension and Nature of Management Accounting Theory in America – An Emphasis on Horngren's Direct Costing Approach', *The Hiroshima Economic Review*, 1991, 3. AA,AJ,3,O

44 Kaname Sakaguchi, 'Die Struktur von Grundrechnung in der Relativen Deckungsbeitragsrechnung' [*'The structure of calculation in relative marginal costing']*, *The Hiroshima Economic Review*, 1991, 3. AA,AJ,1,O

45 Norio Takasu, 'A Characteristic of the Present Historical Cost

Accounting System', *Journal of Business and Economics*, Kinki University, 1991, 7. AA,AJ,1,O

46 Hisashi Kawai, 'A Study of the Environment for the Implementation of DP Chargeback Systems', *The Takachiho Ronso*, 1991, 12. AA,AJ,9,O

47 Hisashi Kawai, 'On Relevance to the Objectives and Selection of DP Chargeback Methods', *The Takachiho Ronso*, 1991, 3. AA,AJ,9,O

48 Fumio Yoshimura, 'Business Budget and Performance Evaluation', *Economic Review*, Kanazawa University, 1991, 3. AA,AJ,5,O

49 Osami Chiba, 'Zum Verhaltnis von Wirklichkeitsnahe Kostenertassung und Wirklichkeit' *['The determination of actual cost reality']*, *Economic Review*, Kanazawa University, 1991, 11. AA,AJ,1,O

50 Misao Yamaguchi, 'Object of Cost Accumulation', *Mita Business Review*, Keio University, 1991, 4. AA,AJ,1,O

51 Soichi Suzuki, 'A Study on the Role of Cost Management in Production Management', *Keieigaku Ronshu*, Nihon Keiei Gakkai, 1991. AA,AJ,1,T

52 Tomoaki Sonoda, 'Cost Allocation of the Master Software Cost', *Mita Business Review*, Keio University, 1991, 6. AA,AJ,1,O

53 Kazumasa Yoshida, 'Cost Accounting Standards (CAS) and Cost Management', *Kenkyu Ronshu*, Hiroshima Keizai University, 1991, 6. AA,AJ,8,O

54 Mutsuko Tokoi, 'Die Eigenschaft des Kostenrechnungs-verstandnis von Schmalenbach (1) – Besonders Uber Seine Gemeinwirtschaftliche Wirtschaftlichkeit' *['The value of understanding Schmalenbach's cost accounting - particularly his non-profit reality']*, *The Kenkyu Ronsyu*, Tokyo Metropolitan College of Commerce, 1991, 3. AA,AJ,1,O

55 Takeo Yoshikawa, 'A Comparative Study of Budgeting Systems in Japan and the UK', *Yokohama Business Review*, 1991, 6. AA,AJ,2,O

References

Anyane-Ntow, K. (1991), 'A Comparison of Budgetary Control Systems in American and Japanese Manufacturing Firms', *Asia Pacific Journal of Management*, October, pp. 201–21.

Bromwich, M. and Bhimani, A. (1989), *Management Accounting: Evolution Not Revolution*, CIMA, London.

Currie, W. (1990), 'Strategic Management of Advanced Manufacturing Technology', *Management Accounting* (UK), October, pp. 50–2.

Currie, W.L. (1991a), 'Managing Production Technology in Japan I', *Management Accounting*, June, pp. 28–9.

Currie, W.L. (1991b), 'Managing Production Technology in Japan II', *Management Accounting*, July, pp. 36–8.

Daniel, S.J. and Reitsperger, W.D. (1992), 'Management Control Systems for Quality: An Empirical Comparison of the US and Japanese Electronics Industries', *Journal of Management Accounting Research*, vol. 4, Fall, pp. 64–78.

Hariman, J.(1990), 'Influencing rather than Informing: Japanese Management Accounting', *Management Accounting* (UK), March, pp. 44–6.

Hiromoto, T. (1988), 'Another Hidden Edge – Japanese Management Accounting', *Harvard Business Review*, July–August, pp. 22–6.

Howell, R.A. and Sakurai, M. (1992), 'Management Accounting (and Other) Lessons from the Japanese', *Management Accounting* (USA), December, pp. 28–34.

Inoue, S. (1988), 'Recent Developments of Cost Management Problems under Technological Changes in Japan', Research Paper No. 30, Kagawa University Department of Information Science, May.

Jinnai, Y. (1990), 'The Function of Accounting: A Japanese Perspective', *Accounting, Auditing and Accountability Journal*, vol. 3, no. 2, pp. 8–23.

Johnson, H.T. (1990), 'Managing Costs versus Managing Activities – Which Strategy Works?', *Financial Executive*, vol. 6, issue 1, January/February, pp. 32–6.

Keyes, D.E. (1991), 'Five Critical Barriers to Successful Implementation of JIT and Total Quality Control', *Industrial Engineering*, vol. 23, no. 1, January, pp. 22–4, 61.

Kharbanda, O.P. (1992), 'Japan's Lessons for the West', *Management Accounting* (USA), February, pp. 26–9.

Kharbanda, O.P. and Stallworthy, E.A. (1991), 'Let's Learn From Japan', *Management Accounting* (UK), March, pp. 26–33.

Kim, I. and Song, J. (1990), 'US, Korea, and Japan: Accounting Practices in Three Countries', *Management Accounting* (USA), vol. 72, no. 2, August, pp. 26–30.

Martin, J.R., Schelb, W.K., Snyder, R.C. and Sparling, J.S. (1992), 'Comparing US and Japanese Companies: Implications for Management Accounting', *Journal of Cost Management for the Manufacturing Industry*, vol. 6, no. 1, Spring, pp. 6–14.

McNair, C.J., Mosconi, W. and Norris, T. (1988), *Meeting the Technology Challenge: Cost Accounting in a JIT Environment*, NAA.

Miyagami, K. (1969), *The Foundations of Business Accounting*, Moriyama Shoten, Tokyo.

Monden, Y. (1992), *Cost Management in the New Manufacturing Age*, Productivity Press, Cambridge, Mass.

Monden, Y. and Hamada, K. (1991), 'Target Costing and Kaizen Costing in Japanese Automobile Companies', *Journal of Management Accounting Research*, vol. 3, Fall, pp. 16–34.

Monden, Y. and Sakurai, M. (eds) (1990), *Japanese Management Accounting: A World Class Approach to Profit Management*, Productivity Press, Cambridge, Mass.

Morgan, M.J. and Weerakoon, P.S.H. (1989), 'Japanese Management Accounting: Its Contribution to the Japanese Economic Miracle', *Management Accounting* (UK), June, pp. 40–3.

Munday, M. (1992), 'A Case of Japanisation', *Management Accounting* (UK), March, pp. 32–3.

Prodhan, B. (1992), 'Ownership and Control: An International Perspective', *Management Accounting* (UK), July/August, pp. 50–3.

Radford, G.D. (1989), 'How Sumitomo Transformed Dunlop Tyres', *Long Range Planning*, June, p. 28 (6 pages).

Sakurai, M. (1989), 'Target Costing and How to Use It', *Journal of Cost Management*, Summer, pp. 39–50.

Sellenheim, M.R. (1991), 'J.I. Case Company: Performance Measurement', *Management Accounting* (USA), September, pp. 50–3.

Tai, S. (1990), 'Managerial Accounting and the "New Managerial Ideas" – A Case Study of the Matsushita Electric Industrial Co. Ltd', *Accounting, Auditing and Accountability Journal*, vol. 3, no. 2, pp. 52–65.

Taylor, A. (1993), 'How Toyota Copes With Hard Times', *Fortune*, 25 January , pp. 78–81.

Thackray, P. (1990), 'The Issue is Quality', *Management Accounting* (UK), November, pp. 50–1.

Williams, J., Haslan, C. and Williams, K. (1990), 'Bad Work Practices and Good Management Practices: The Consequences of the Extension of Managerial Control in British and Japanese Manufacturing Since 1950', *Business History Review*, vol. 64, issue 4, Winter, pp. 657–88.

Worthy, F.S. (1991), 'Japan's Smart Secret Weapon', *Fortune*, vol. 124, issue 4, 12 August, pp. 72–5.

Yoshikawa, T., Innes, J. and Mitchell, F. (1989a), 'Cost Management through Functional Analysis', *Journal of Cost Management*, Spring, pp. 14–19.

Yoshikawa, T., Innes, J. and Mitchell, F. (1989b), 'Japanese Management Accounting: a Comparative Survey', *Management Accounting*, November, pp. 20–3.

Yoshikawa, T., Innes, J. and Mitchell, F. (1990), 'Cost Tables: A Foundation of Japanese Cost Management', *Journal of Cost Management*, Fall, pp. 30–6.

Yoshikawa, T., Innes, J. and Mitchell, F. (1993), 'Japanese Cost Management Practices', in B. Brinker (ed.), *Handbook of Cost Management*, Warren, Gorham & Lamont, Boston.

Yoshikawa, T., Innes, J., Mitchell, F. and Tanaka, M., *Contemporary Cost Management*, Chapman & Hall, London.